PRAGMATISM

From Peirce to Davidson

John P. Murphy

WITH AN INTRODUCTION BY

Richard Rorty

Westview Press
BOULDER • SAN FRANCISCO • OXFORD

Published in 1990 in the United States of America by Westview Press, Inc., 5500 Central Avenue, Boulder, Colorado 80301, and in the United Kingdom by Westview Press, 36 Lonsdale Road, Summertown, Oxford OX2 7EW

Library of Congress Cataloging-in-Publication Data
Murphy, John P. (John Peter), 1937–1987.
  Pragmatism : from Peirce to Davidson / John P. Murphy :
with an introduction by Richard Rorty.
    p. cm.
  Includes index.
  ISBN 0-8133-7809-5 — ISBN 0-8133-7810-9 (pbk.)
  1. Pragmatism—History. 2. Philosophy, American—20th century.
I. Rorty, Richard. II. Title.
B944.P72M87 1990
144'.3—dc20   89-9008
                                                                              CIP

Printed and bound in the United States of America

The paper used in this publication meets the requirements
of the American National Standard for Permanence of Paper
for Printed Library Materials Z39.48-1984.

10   9   8   7   6   5   4   3   2   1

CONTENTS

As part of a curriculum revision project undertaken by the Trinity University Philosophy Department, the late Professor John Murphy undertook the development of an undergraduate course on pragmatism. Thanks to a generous grant from the National Endowment for the Humanities, Professor Murphy was able to take the time to read widely in the area and then to write this book. While he was working on this project, he and I discussed some of the relevant issues. When he had finished the manuscript, he sent me a copy. It seemed to me that he had managed to tell an extraordinarily clear and coherent story about pragmatism in a very brief compass—a story that exhibited the relations between Peirce, James, Dewey, Quine, and Davidson in a very illuminating way. I looked forward to the publication of the book because I wanted to use it in my teaching.

However, Professor Murphy's tragically early death occurred not long after he had finished the manuscript. With the encouragement of his widow and of his colleagues, I edited the manuscript for publication by Westview Press. This task was largely a matter of making minor changes in format; apart from these changes and the correction of typographical errors, I have meddled very little with what Professor Murphy wrote. I am not sure that he would have agreed with everything I wrote in my Introduction to the book, but I think that he would have accepted its general drift.

Meredith Garmon and I have added a Bibliography that lists, section by section, the readings in primary sources that Professor Murphy included in his proposed course syllabus and that his commentary is designed to accompany. As an aid to those who wish to use this book as a text, we have included some information about alternative books (mostly paperback anthologies) in which some of these readings can be found. We have also listed various other primary and secondary sources that teachers and students of pragmatism may wish to consult.

Richard Rorty
University of Virginia

Pragmatism as Anti-Representationalism

RICHARD RORTY

There is still an air of provincialism about pragmatism. Peirce, James, and Dewey are studied mainly in their native land, the United States. Philosophers in Britain often rely on Bertrand Russell's rather contemptuous treatment of James's and Dewey's thought in *The History of Western Philosophy*. Philosophers in France, Germany, and Italy often discuss Peirce as one of the founders of the study of signs, but they rarely follow up on the leads that James and Dewey found in Peirce. Though philosophers in all these countries study Quine and Davidson, they tend to shrug off the suggestion that these contemporary philosophers of language share their basic outlook with American philosophers who wrote prior to the so-called linguistic turn. Again, just as many analytic philosophers are content to shrug off pragmatism as pre-linguistic, many "continental" philosophers are willing to take Heidegger's word for it that "the American interpretation of Americanism by means of pragmatism still remains outside the metaphysical realm."[1]

It is unlikely that Heidegger meant that cryptic sentence as a compliment. For Heidegger, the metaphysical realm was pervaded by the Greek philosophers' distinction between appearance and reality. Heidegger thought that the Greek understanding of Being had culminated in our contemporary technological culture—a culture in which everything is viewed as an exploitable resource and of which "Americanism" is paradigmatic. So his remark about pragmatism probably meant that Americans are so primitive that their understanding of their own technological frenzy does not even take a respectably philosophical form.

But one *could* take Heidegger to be paying pragmatism a compliment. One might read him as saying that America is still, happily, innocent of metaphysics, for it has not yet become caught up in the disastrous appearance/reality distinction. Most of the American philosophers discussed in this book share a desire to eschew that distinction. Dewey thought that the Greeks saddled the philosophical tradition with the view that "the empirical world in which we live from day to day is crass and obdurate, stubbornly un-ideal in character because it is only an appearance of the reality of which thought is the author."[2] Dewey was equally impatient with "scientific realism," the notion that empirical scientific research can tell us about a reality that is what it is apart from human needs and interests: "Only when the older (i.e., Greek) theory of knowledge and metaphysics is retained, is science thought to inform us that nature in true reality is but an interplay of masses in motion, without sound, color, or any quality of experience or use."[3]

Only what Dewey called a spectator theory of knowledge can lead one to think that metaphysics, empirical science, or some other discipline might someday penetrate through the veil of appearances and allow us to glimpse things as they are in themselves. For that theory assumes that there is something like what Hilary Putnam called a "God's-eye view" of things.[4] A God's-eye view is one that is irrelevant to our needs and our practices. Such a view would, in Bernard Williams's words, "represent the world in a way to the maximum degree independent of our perspective and its peculiarities."[5]

Anti-pragmatist writers such as Williams believe that "there is clearly such a thing as practical reasoning or deliberation, which is not the same as thinking about how things are. It is *obviously* not the same. . . ."[6] Dewey spent his life trying to blur the distinction that Williams thinks sharp, trying to render Williams's claim inobvious. Taking his cue from Peirce's use of Alexander Bain's definition of belief, Dewey dismissed the idea that beliefs represent reality. He tried to substitute the idea that beliefs are tools for dealing with reality—maxims dictating the behavior of the organism that has the belief.

Anti-representationalism—the abandonment of a "spectator" account of knowledge and the consequent abandonment of the appearance/reality distinction—is the theme that runs through Professor Murphy's book. Davidson recently offered a brisk and comprehensive restatement of this theme: "Beliefs are true or false, but they represent nothing. It is good to be rid of representations, and with them the correspondence theory of truth, for it is thinking that there are representations that engenders thoughts of relativism. Representations *are* relative to a scheme: a map represents Mexico, say—but only relative to a mercator, or some other, projection."[7] Davidson's last sentence is an effective rejoinder to the charge that relativism is the only alternative to Williams's Locke-like distinction between how things are independently of us and how we describe things in order to serve our needs. Davidson meets this familiar charge by saying that whether inscriptions or utterances count as true will, indeed, depend in part upon which language they are taken as statements in. That sort of relativity, however, is no more dangerous than the fact that any representation of a sphere on a plane must have its accuracy judged relative to the mercator or some other projection. To hope for absoluteness, however, would be to hope for something analogous to the claim that, for example, the mercator projection is truest to the way the sphere really is. It would also be to hope to justify some such claim as that, for example, the language of physics is truest to how things really are in themselves.

In the case of maps one *can* make some sense of such a claim. One can, for example, say that a certain projection produces maps of the hemispheres that are more reminiscent of the view from a moon rocket than maps using other projections. But what could be the analogue to that view in the case of a choice of descriptive vocabularies? The only such analogue, Putnam argued, is something like "the view from God's eye"—what Thomas Nagel calls "the view from nowhere." Philosophers like Nagel and Williams think that the notion of such a view, and of a language that embodies such a view, is a useful one. Most of the authors discussed in this book do not.

Rather, most of these authors see the appearance/reality distinction as J. L. Austin saw it—as useful when confined to relatively narrow contexts (apparent magnitude rather than real magnitude, non-dairy creamer rather than real cream), but useless when blown up to the traditional philosophical scale. For them, it is useless to ask whether one vocabulary rather than another is closer to reality. For different vocabularies serve different purposes, and there is no such thing as a purpose that is closer to reality than another purpose. In particular, there is no purpose that is simply "finding out how things are" as opposed to finding out how to predict their motion, explain their behavior, and so on. Nothing is conveyed by saying, with Locke and Williams, that the vocabulary in which we predict the motion of a planet is more in touch with how things really are than the vocabulary in which we assign the planet an astrological influence. For to say that astrology is out of touch with reality cannot *explain* why astrology is useless; it merely restates that fact in misleading representationalist terms.

Philosophers such as Davidson have doubts about even the modest attempts of Peirce and Putnam to find "absolute" senses for the words *reality* and *truth*. Despite his alliance with Bain and his attacks on Descartes, Peirce was still attached to the notion of representation, and he employs it when he says "The opinion which is fated to be ultimately agreed to by all who investigate is what we mean by the truth, and the object represented in this opinion is the real."[8] Despite the fact that he follows Nelson Goodman in abandoning the idea that there is a Way The World Is, Putnam entitles his most recent book *Representation and Reality*. He still offers "idealized rational acceptability" as a useful definition of truth.[9]

For those who, like myself, accept Davidson's more thoroughgoing repudiation of representationalist notions, Peirce's term "fated to be ultimately agreed to" and Putnam's term "idealized" are suspicious. We doubt that these terms can be cashed out into anything that will clarify the notion of "absolute truth" or "absolute reality." For we doubt that there is a single project called inquiry, which might be thought of as coming to a fated end. We also doubt that there is a single ideal in terms of which to define "ideal acceptability." Because we do not think of "finding out how things are" or "discovering truth" as a distinct human project, Peirce's and Putnam's "end of inquiry" versions of absolutism seem to us misguided.

Both attempts, it appears to us, share Locke's and Williams's unfortunate desire to privilege the language of natural science over other vocabularies—to see natural science as something more than another tool for accomplishing various human purposes. We heartily agree with Putnam's diagnosis of logical empiricism as "hypnotized by the success of science to such an extent that it could not conceive of the possibility of knowledge and reason outside of what we are pleased to call the sciences,"[10] but we think that Putnam himself is still occasionally so hypnotized. For if he were not, why would he think that what he calls "the quest for human flourishing" will converge to a *single* description of the world in the way in which communities of problem-solving scientists converge on a single solution to a given problem? Why would he share Peirce's vision of such convergence? And why would he worry about "cultural relativism" rather than, like Davidson, urging that the problematic of relativism and absolutism be set aside?[11]

From the radically anti-representationalist viewpoint I am commending, pragmatism can be seen as gradually emerging, in the course of a century or so, from the hypnotic trance Putnam describes. It has gradually been escaping from scientism. Signs of this escape include Davidson's criticism of Quine's obstinately physicalistic ontology as "adventitious philosophical puritanism" and his repeated criticisms of Quine's attempt to save something of the traditional empiricist idea that, as Quine wrote, "surface irritations . . . exhaust our clues to the external world."[12] Pragmatism has gradually broken the historical links that once connected it to empiricism and utilitarianism, links that still make it seem (especially to philosophers such as Heidegger, Adorno, Habermas, and Foucault) like one more celebration of what Habermas calls technical reason.

From this point of view, the best and purest representatives of pragmatism—those least infected with reductionistic thinking—are Dewey and Davidson. When they criticize traditional dualisms (Platonic, Cartesian, Kantian), they are almost entirely free of the temptation to find an Archimedean point from which to launch their criticisms—a point that is located on the "reality" side of the appearance/reality distinction. They are also almost entirely free of the temptation to suggest that their own philosophical views represent things as they are in themselves.

In the past, philosophers who have tried to overcome representationalism have typically succumbed to this temptation: Nietzsche, Bergson, Whitehead, and Heidegger are notorious examples. By contrast, Dewey and Davidson are content to take up one traditional dualism after another, point to the difficulties to which it has led, and suggest that we can do without it. This is a relatively undramatic way of doing philosophy. The lack of high drama in their work helps account for the persistent belief that Dewey was merely a prolix and prosaic bore and for the persistent attempts to affix labels to Davidson ("realist," "anti-realist"), which he must then patiently scrape off.

As Murphy and I tell the story of pragmatism, what Davidson added to Dewey is a non-representationalist philosophy of language that supplements, and in some measure replaces, Dewey's non-representationalist account of knowledge. I have argued elsewhere that the "linguistic turn" in philosophy was a sort of last refuge of representationalism and that the dialectic that leads the later Wittgenstein and Davidson away from a picture theory of language is the same as that which led Dewey away from a spectator theory of knowledge.[13] If no further refuge is found, then Davidson may have been right when he wrote that "a sea change" is occurring in recent philosophical thought—"a change so profound that we may not recognize that it is occurring."[14] If the change of which Davidson spoke is someday recognized as having occurred, the authors whom Professor Murphy discussed in this book will get a good deal of the credit for bringing it about. Given such recognition, Peirce, James, and Dewey may cease to be treated as provincial figures. They may be given the place I think they deserve in the story of the West's intellectual progress.

NOTES

1. Martin Heidegger, *The Question Concerning Technology and Other Essays*, trans. William Lovitt (New York: Harper and Row, 1977), p. 153. The original can be found at *Holzwege* (Frankfurt: Klostermann, 1972), pp. 103–104.

2. John Dewey, *The Quest for Certainty* (New York: Putnam, 1960), p. 108.

3. *Ibid.*, p. 104.

4. Putnam is one of the most important contributors to contemporary pragmatism, but in order to keep his course syllabus to a manageable size, Professor Murphy did not discuss Putnam's work in this book. For the same reason he failed to discuss such influential pragmatists as F.C.S. Schiller, George Herbert Mead, C. I. Lewis, Sidney Hook, and Nelson Goodman. For a discussion of pragmatism that incorporates Schiller, Mead, and Lewis, see H. S. Thayer, *Meaning and Action: A Critical History of Pragmatism* (New York: Bobbs-Merrill, 1968). For a discussion of Hook, see Cornel West, *The American Avoidance of Philosophy: A Genealogy of Pragmatism* (Madison: University of Wisconsin Press, 1988).

5. Bernard Williams, *Ethics and the Limits of Philosophy* (Cambridge, Mass.: Harvard U.P., 1985), pp. 138–139.

6. Ibid., p. 135. For a reply to Williams from a pragmatist perspective, see Richard Rorty, "Is Natural Science a Natural Kind?" in *Construction and Constraint: The Shaping of Scientific Rationality*, ed. E. McMullin (Notre Dame, Ind.: Notre Dame University Press, 1988), pp. 49–74.

7. Donald Davidson, "The Myth of the Subjective," *Relativism: Interpretation and Confrontation*, ed. Michael Krausz (Notre Dame, Ind.: Notre Dame University Press, 1989), pp. 165–166.

8. *Philosophical Writings of Peirce*, ed. Justus Buchler (New York: Dover, 1955), p. 38.

9. See Hilary Putnam, *Representation and Reality* (Cambridge, Mass.: MIT Press, 1988), p. 115.

10. Hilary Putnam, *Reason, Truth and History* (Cambridge: Cambridge University Press, 1981), p. 185.

11. Even James, the least scientistic of the pragmatists and the most sympathetic to religious belief, falls into scientistic rhetoric at the beginning of *Pragmatism* when he talks about the pragmatists' "tough-mindedness." I have argued— though this is a matter of much dispute—that Dewey's constant praise of the scientific method was not an instance of what Putnam condemns or a suggestion that natural science somehow gets closer to the way things are than other areas of culture, but merely praise for certain moral virtues typically exhibited by natural scientists. See my Introduction to *John Dewey: The Later Works, vol. 8: 1933*, ed. Jo Ann Boydston (Carbondale: Southern Illinois University Press, 1986), ix–xviii, my "Comments on Sleeper and Edel," *Transactions of The Charles S. Peirce Society* 21 (Winter 1985), 40–48, and the closing pages of "Is Natural Science a Natural Kind?" cited in note 6 above.

12. Willard Quine, *Word and Object* (Cambridge, Mass.: MIT Press, 1960), p. 22. For Davidson's latest criticism of Quine's residual sympathy with Locke, see his "Meaning, Truth and Evidence," forthcoming in the proceedings of the 1988 St. Louis Quine conference.

13. See my *Philosophy and the Mirror of Nature* (Princeton, N.J.: Princeton University Press, 1979), chapter 6. On the Davidson-Wittgenstein parallel, see my "Heidegger, Wittgenstein and the Reification of Language," forthcoming in *The Cambridge Companion to Heidegger*, ed. Charles Guignon.

14. Davidson, "The Myth of the Subjective," p. 159.

CHAPTER ONE

Charles Peirce's Rejection of Cartesianism

Charles Sanders Peirce is the founder of pragmatism. He was born in Cambridge, Massachusetts, in 1839. His father, Benjamin Peirce, was a distinguished professor of mathematics and astronomy at Harvard. Born and bred in a scientific environment, Charles Peirce showed great promise in mathematics and the experimental sciences from his earliest years. According to his own account, he may almost be said to have lived in a laboratory from the age of six until long past maturity. Thus, raised as "an experimentalist" and having all his life associated mostly with experimentalists, he always had a confident sense of understanding and being understood by those whose minds were likewise molded by laboratory life. This was so long before he entered Harvard as a student in 1855, so it seems likely that it was the attitude he took to Harvard.

But Harvard, in the 1850's, was not a place to bring such an experimentalist attitude toward the study of philosophy. Despite the fact that Chauncey Wright, Nicolas St. John Green, and Oliver Wendell Holmes, Jr., as well as Peirce, studied in the Department of "Intellectual and Moral Philosophy" during that decade, a committee of the Harvard Board of Overseers reported in January 1860, that there was "a great deficiency in this department," that it was in "a neglected and destitute condition."[1] According to that report, instruction in metaphysics, logic, ethics, and natural and revealed theology had been "curtailed, cut down, and driven out step by step from its proper place in the College course."[2] The study of philosophy at Harvard in the 1850's was "brief and hurried," "an exercise of memory more than understanding."[3] Imagine how desultory this must have seemed to a sixteen-year-old scientific prodigy who had already studied Kant's *Critique of Pure Reason* for over three years under his father's tutelage! Peirce received his B.A. from Harvard in 1859. He graduated seventy-first in a class of ninety-one.

While reading Kant, Peirce sometimes "came upon strains of thought that recalled the ways of thinking of the laboratory."[4] So he felt he might "trust to" Kant.[5] As a consequence of this, his industry, and his genius, the teenage Peirce became so deeply imbued with many of Kant's ways of thinking that he was never able to free himself of them. "When I was a babe in philosophy my bottle was filled from the udders of Kant," he wrote in 1860.[6] Thinking back to his Harvard days, I presume, he goes on to say that his attitude toward the study of Kant was always "that of a dweller in a laboratory, eager only to learn what he did not know, and not that of philosophers bred in theological seminaries, whose ruling impulse is to teach what they hold to be infallibly true."[7]

A year after receiving his B.A., Peirce read Darwin's *Origin of Species* while surveying the wilds of Louisiana for the United States Coast and Geodetic Survey, whose permanent staff he joined the following year. In 1862, he received his M.A. from Harvard while matriculating at the Lawrence Scientific School, where he earned his Sc.B. in chemistry *summa cum laude* the following year. In 1864–1865, Peirce lectured on the philosophy of science at Harvard. In 1866, he began his pioneering researches in mathematical logic, a subject that became a lifelong preoccupation with him. Throughout the 1860's, Peirce was greatly stimulated by the thoughts of two other students of Darwin's evolutionary thinking: Chauncey Wright (Harvard, 1852), who was on the verge of being considered something of a philosophic sage in Cambridge; and Peirce's Harvard classmate, Frank Abbot, who, like Wright, regarded Descartes as the thinker who had put modern philosophy on the wrong road, the road to skepticism. Peirce added his voice to this anti-Cartesian chorus in a pair of articles that appeared in the *Journal of Speculative Philosophy* in 1868.

The term Cartesianism is ambiguous. Descartes had made an ambitious attempt to reconstitute human knowledge. His contemporaries and successors developed this attempt in various directions. One line of development, as *The Encyclopedia of Philosophy* puts it,

> can be traced from Descartes' novel use of the term *idea* in presenting what has sometimes been considered the characteristically Cartesian view that knowledge is attained by way of ideas. These "as it were images of things," as they were introduced in the *Third Meditation*, were variously described in his works, and a host of questions arose about their origin and nature. . . . Since Locke and his followers accepted Descartes' general thesis although they disagreed on the subject of innate ideas, Cartesianism,

in [this] application of the term, has been taken to cover a considerably wider domain . . .[8]

By "Cartesianism," we will always mean Cartesianism in this broad application of the term; an application in which, as Peirce says, "most modern philosophers have been, in effect, Cartesians."[9] That is why Descartes is said to be the father of modern philosophy.

He was the first philosopher to get what Quine would later call "the idea idea."[10] Adventitious ideas, for Descartes, are mental images or mental pictures; that is, pictures that are on display in an inner space called the mind. All thought has ideas as objects. This is a totally new perspective in the history of philosophy, and Locke's quick acceptance of it—his use of "idea" to refer to whatever is the object of the understanding when a man thinks—made it the key term of modern philosophy even though, as Rorty points out,

the modern use of the word *idea* derives through Locke from Descartes. As Anthony Kenny puts it, "Descartes was consciously giving it a new sense. . . it was a new departure to use it systematically for the contents of a human mind." More importantly, there had been no term, even of philosophical art, in the Greek and medieval traditions coextensive with the Descartes-Locke use of "idea." Nor had there been the conception of the human mind as an inner space in which both pains and clear and distinct ideas passed in review before a single Inner Eye. There were, to be sure, the notions of taking tacit thought, forming resolutions in *foro interno*, and the like. The novelty was the notion of a single inner space in which bodily and perceptual sensations ('confused ideas of sense and imagination' in Descartes' phrase), mathematical truths, moral rules, the idea of God, moods of depression, and all the rest of what we now call "mental" were objects of quasi-observation. Such an inner arena with its inner observer had been suggested at various points in ancient and medieval thought but it had never been taken seriously long enough to form the basis for a problematic. But the seventeenth century took it seriously enough to permit it to pose the problem of the veil of ideas, the problem which made epistemology central to philosophy.[11]

To have the idea idea is to believe that we have a power of introspection—an ability to focus the eye of the mind on the ideas within one's mental space, so as to determine the contents of the mind. And, as Descartes develops the idea, it is to assume that we have an intuitive faculty for distinguishing between those ideas that "are determined by" other ideas (Peirce calls them "mediate cognitions") and those that are not (Peirce's "intuitive cognitions"). Determination is best thought of as a consequence relation: Idea A is determined by ideas $B_1, \ldots , B_n$, if and only if some sentence that means A is a logical consequence of a set of sentences that mean $B_1, \ldots, B_n$, respectively.

In an essay of 1868, "Questions Concerning Certain Faculties Claimed for Man," Peirce argues (among other things) that we have neither of these faculties. We have no power of introspection; our whole knowledge of the internal world is derived from the observation of external facts. And we have no power of intuition. In particular, we have no intuitive faculty for knowing our own existence. *Contra* Descartes, that knowledge too is determined by other ideas. And, more generally, we have no intuitive faculty for knowing that certain ideas are not determined by any others.

In a sequel published in the same year, "Some Consequences of Four Incapacities," Peirce argues that "we have no images even in actual perception." In Section 1, Peirce describes "the spirit of Cartesianism" as follows:

> Descartes is the father of modern philosophy, and the spirit of Cartesianism—that which principally distinguishes it from the scholasticism which it displaced—may be compendiously stated as follows:
>
> 1. It teaches that philosophy must begin with universal doubt; whereas scholasticism had never questioned fundamentals.
> 2. It teaches that the ultimate test of certainty is to be found in the individual consciousness; whereas scholasticism had rested on the testimony of sages and of the Catholic Church.
> 3. The multiform argumentation of the middle ages is replaced by a single thread of inference depending often upon inconspicuous premisses.
> 4. Scholasticism had its mysteries of faith, but undertook to explain all created things. But there are many facts which Cartesianism not only does not explain but renders absolutely inexplicable, unless to say that "God makes them so" is to be regarded as an explanation.
>
> In some, or all of these respects, most modern philosophers have been, in effect, Cartesians. Now without wishing to return to scholasticism, it seems to me that modern science and modern logic require us to stand upon a very different platform from this.[12]

When this was published, Charles Sanders Peirce was twenty-nine years old. There was probably no one in the world better qualified than he to talk about the philosophical platform that "modern science and modern logic require us to stand upon." For example, his discovery of abduction as a third fundamental mode of inference (along with induction and deduction) and his publication of "Upon the Logic of Mathematics" in the *Proceedings of the American Academy of Arts and Sciences* had already been accomplished when this critique of the spirit of Cartesianism was made.

Peirce opposes the spirit of Cartesianism with what might be called the spirit of experimentalism. This spirit has the following three characteristics:

1. *It denies that philosophy must begin with universal doubt:*

> We cannot begin with complete doubt. We must begin with all the prejudices which we actually have when we enter upon the study of philosophy. These prejudices are not to be dispelled by a maxim, for they are things which it does not occur to us *can* be questioned. Hence this initial scepticism will be a mere self-deception, and not real doubt; and no one who follows the Cartesian method will ever be satisfied until he has formally recovered all those beliefs which in form he has given up. It is, therefore, as useless a preliminary as going to the North Pole would be in order to get to Constantinople by coming down regularly on a meridian. A person may, it is true, in the course of his studies, find reason to doubt what he began by believing; but in that case he doubts because he has a positive reason for it, and not on account of the Cartesian maxim. Let us not pretend to doubt in philosophy what we do not doubt in our hearts.[13]

There's a difference between simply saying "I doubt that there are mountains in Colorado" and actually doubting that there are mountains in Colorado. When one has a genuine doubt, one has a reason to doubt. He is then in a position to make an inquiry concerning whether or not it is a *good* reason for doubt. If it is not, the doubt is allayed; if it is a good reason, the doubt is reinforced and further inquiry may lead to actual disbelief. But if one seeks to begin an inquiry simply by saying "I doubt that there are mountains in Colorado" without giving any *specific reason* for entertaining this *specific doubt*, one is at a loss to know how to proceed. I can only show you that your reason for doubting that there are mountains in Colorado isn't a good reason if you have a reason for doubting that fact.

2. *The spirit of experimentalism denies that the ultimate test of certainty is to be found in the individual consciousness:*

> The same formalism appears in the Cartesian criterion, which amounts to this: "Whatever I am clearly convinced of, is true." If I were really convinced, I should have done with reasoning and should require no test of certainty. But thus to make single individuals absolute judges of truth is most pernicious. The result is that metaphysicians will all agree that metaphysics has reached a pitch of certainty far beyond that of the physical

sciences;—only they can agree upon nothing else. In sciences in which men come to agreement, when a theory has been broached it is considered to be on probation until this agreement is reached. After it is reached, the question of certainty becomes an idle one, because there is no one left who doubts it. We individually cannot reasonably hope to attain the ultimate philosophy which we pursue; we can only seek it, therefore, for the *community* of philosophers. Hence, if disciplined and candid minds carefully examine a theory and refuse to accept it, this ought to create doubts in the mind of the author of the theory himself.[14]

Peirce was seeking to turn philosophy into one of those "sciences in which men come to agreement." Where that has been accomplished, one can speak of knowledge, truth, and reality, but these concepts will be grounded in the *community* of inquirers, not in the individual consciousness. Here we see the roots of Peirce's so-called limit theory of truth—in a communitarian idealism, which represents the presuppositions of scientific method as to some extent dictating the nature of reality.

3. *The spirit of experimentalism denies that a philosophical theory should be a single thread of inference, in the manner of Descartes:*

Philosophy ought to imitate the successful sciences in its methods, so far as to proceed only from tangible premises which can be subjected to careful scrutiny, and to trust rather to the multitude and variety of its arguments than to the conclusiveness of any one. Its reasoning should not form a chain which is no stronger than its weakest link, but a cable whose fibers may be ever so slender, provided they are sufficiently numerous and intimately connected.[15]

There is here an implicit rejection of the Cartesian concept of experience—the veil of ideas, the veil of Maya. Experience, as conceived by the experimentalist, is something tangible. It reaches right down into nature; it has depth. As John Dewey writes, "experience, if scientific inquiry is justified, is no infinitesimally thin layer or foreground of nature, . . . it penetrates into it, reaching down into its depths, and in such a way that its grasp is capable of expansion; it tunnels in all directions and in so doing brings to the surface things at first hidden— as miners pile high on the surface of the earth treasures brought from below."[16] This is Peirce's point as well. And there was no question in his mind that scientific inquiry *is* justified. As regards methodology, philosophy should imitate, rather than criticize, the successful sciences.

CHAPTER TWO

William James's Teleological Theory of Mind

William James was three years younger than Charles Peirce. He was the oldest son of Henry James the elder, a religious writer (a Swedenborgian) of independent means, and a literary associate of Oliver Wendell Holmes, Sr., and Ralph Waldo Emerson. James had four siblings, the oldest being Henry James, Jr., the novelist. William had become interested in science at an early age, and, later, painting. His formal education took place irregularly and in a great variety of private establishments. Between 1855 and 1860, William (and Henry) attended schools in England, France, Switzerland, and Germany. There William divided his interests between natural science and painting.

When he decided to become an artist in 1860, his father brought him back from Paris and arranged for him to study painting under the influential painter of the Barbizon School, William Morris Hunt of Newport, Rhode Island. In the fall of 1861, James gave up painting and entered the Lawrence Scientific School, where he studied chemistry and then comparative anatomy and physiology. Two years later, he entered Harvard Medical School, where his studies, "although fruitful, were attenuated and sporadic."[1] He did not receive his M.D. until 1869. It was at the Lawrence Scientific School that he met Charles Peirce, whom he suspected "to be a very 'smart' fellow with a great deal of character, pretty independent and violent though."[2] From the early 1860's, James associated with a whole group of Cambridge intellectuals in addition to Peirce—Chauncey Wright, Oliver Wendell Holmes, Jr., John Fiske (who would soon gain a reputation as an articulate defender of Herbert Spencer's evolutionary thought), John Chipman Gray (a lawyer and friend of Holmes), Nicholas St. John Green (a colleague of Holmes at Harvard

Law School), and Peirce's friends and protégés, Frank Abbot and Joseph B. Warner.

One of James's teachers at the Lawrence Scientific School was Louis Agassiz, the leading zoologist in America, who had also become this country's principal critic of Darwin's theory of evolution by natural selection. In March, 1865, James left medical school to go on an expedition to Brazil under Agassiz's leadership. Those nine months on the Amazon with Agassiz made the Darwinian controversy a personal one for James. They also seem to have had a therapeutic effect on him. James had always suffered from what his chemistry teacher, Charles Eliot, termed "a delicacy of nervous condition,"[3] and, in recent years, he had been becoming quite a hypochondriac.

Nonetheless, he returned from Brazil in excellent physical condition and resumed his medical studies—but not for long. He was soon plagued by severe back pains and, in the spring of 1867, decided to go to Germany to try a cure of mineral baths at Nauheim, in Bohemia, and to study psychology in the German laboratories. The baths did little good for James's back pains, and he didn't feel able to undertake laboratory work. But he managed to hear some lectures at the University of Berlin and to read the latest German books on physiology and psychology as well as the German publications of the experiments conducted in Wundt's psychology laboratory at Heidelberg. For the first time, James began to think of becoming a psychologist.

But philosophy was never far from his thoughts either. He wrote from Berlin to his Cambridge friend Oliver Wendell Holmes, Jr., in January 1868: "When I get home let's establish a philosophical society to have regular meetings and discuss none but the tallest and broadest questions. . . . It will give each one a chance to air his own opinion in a grammatical form, and to sneer and chuckle when he goes home at what damned fools all the other members are—and may grow into something very important after a sufficient number of years."[4]

Such was the origin of what came to be called The Metaphysical Club, which flourished in Cambridge in the early 1870's. As James wrote to Holmes, it was "to be composed of none but the very topmost cream of Boston manhood."[5] The core of the club, in addition to James and Holmes, consisted of Charles Peirce, Chauncey Wright, Nicholas St. John Green, and Joseph Warner. Six others were more peripherally connected: Frank Abbot, John Fiske, John Chipman Gray, William Montague, Henry Putnam, and Francis Greenwood Peabody. Bruce Kuklick, in his *The Rise of American Philosophy*, describes the group as follows:

The men were Harvard educated exclusively; with the exception of William James, each had a Harvard B.A. They were young—the average age was thirty-three—but there were three distinct age groupings: Green and Wright had received their degrees in 1851 and 1852 respectively; five others— Abbot, Fiske, Gray, Holmes, and Peirce (peers of James)—received degrees between 1859 and 1863; the remaining four were all class of 1869. They were practical men; of the six core members three were lawyers, three scientists. Of the wider group, six were lawyers, three scientists, two theologians, and one librarian (by courtesy only—Fiske's main source of support, in addition to contributions from his family, was writing and lecturing).[6]

When the club was in full swing, Henry James wrote to a friend that William and "various other long-headed youths have combined to form a Metaphysical Club, where they wrangle grimly and stick to the question. It gives me a headache merely to know of it."[7]

When James returned from Europe in the fall of 1868, he was in worse health than when he left. Perhaps that was why The Metaphysical Club did not get going for another two or three years. Actually, James would spend the next four years as a semi-invalid. Despite the fact that he finished his medical school thesis and all other requirements for the M.D. during the 1868–1869 academic year, there was no abatement of James's various neurotic symptoms. At that time, he had been studying Herbert Spencer's evolutionary philosophy for about eight years. In 1868, he was struggling with the problem of justifying "a spiritual orientation to life" within (what he then thought of as) such a scientific worldview (of justifying it, for example, to Chauncey Wright).

"During the winter of 1869–1870, James labored under a sense of frustration, despair, and impotence. Day after day, he awoke with a feeling of 'horrible dread',"[8] and it is clear that he was undergoing "a profound emotional crisis."[9] He seemed "to be declining into a desultory and profitless idleness."[10] James was himself beginning to suspect that his various ailments were, as we would say, psychosomatic. And he was determined to get well. He suspected that recovery depended to a large extent on his own willpower; but there was the philosophical rub: How could he decide to exercise his will if the world was deterministic, as Spencer and Fiske had convinced him that it was?

Fortunately, since his return from Europe, James had been reading the philosophical essays of the French neo-Kantian, Charles Renouvier. James's diary for April 30, 1870, contains the following entry:

I think that yesterday was a crisis in my life. I finished the first part of Renouvier's second *Essais* and see no reason why his definition of free will—"the sustaining of a thought *because I choose to* when I might have other thoughts"—need be the definition of an illusion. At any rate, I will assume for the present—until next year—that it is no illusion. My first act of free will shall be to believe in free will.[11]

There was no room for free will in the system of Herbert Spencer, who modeled the mind as a complex mechanical system, operating on principles like those accepted in the physical sciences. So, according to James, Spencer must be wrong: Free will, in at least one interesting sense of the term, is a distinct possibility. To actualize that possibility, James would have to find a place for it in a "fundamental and well-established" model of mind.[12] James spent the years between 1878 and 1890 working on his two volume *Principles of Psychology*, wherein what Renouvier called free will, "the sustaining of a thought because one chooses to have when one might have other thoughts," is integrated into (indeed, dominates) a so-called reflex theory of mind. This theory takes the structured unit of the nervous system to be a triad of perception (which conveys what is given in experience), thinking (which displays consciousness), and will (which indicates mind itself):

> The sensory impression exists only for the sake of awaking the central process of reflection, and the central process of reflection exists only for the sake of calling forth the final act. All action is thus reaction upon the outer world; and the middle stage of consideration or contemplation or thinking is only a place of transit, the bottom of a loop, both whose ends have their point of application in the outer world. If it should ever have no roots in the outer world, if it should ever happen that it led to no active measures, it would fail of its essential function, and would have to be considered either pathological or abortive. The current of life which runs in at our eyes or ears is meant to run out at our hands, feet, or lips. The only use of the thoughts it occasions while inside is to determine its direction to whichever of these organs shall, on the whole, under the circumstances actually present, act in the way most propitious to our welfare. The willing department of our nature, in short, dominates both the conceiving department and the feeling compartment; or, in plainer English, perception and thinking are only there for behavior's sake.[13]

This was James's solution to his principal problem in the 1880's. But we must return to the spring of 1870, when it was all James could do to lift himself out of his depression by the strength of his own will. He resolved to refrain from all "speculative brooding" for the rest of 1870 and to read only books that would strengthen his new-found confidence in his freedom to act.[14]

This strategy seems to have been quite successful. James's former chemistry teacher, Charles Eliot, had become president of Harvard in 1869; and, in 1872, he felt that James had recovered sufficiently to be appointed to an instructorship in anatomy and physiology. This was "a perfect God-send" for James.[15] "It is a noble thing for one's spirits to have some responsible work to do."[16] In 1875, James began teaching psychology, and the following year, he was appointed to an assistant professorship of physiology. In 1878, when "Remarks on Spencer's Definition of Mind as Correspondence," was published, James finally married. His wife has been described as a supportive and self-sacrificing woman who devoted herself to keeping him intact. "I have found in marriage," James wrote, "a calm and repose I never knew before."[17] During that same year, he began working on *Principles of Psychology*, a task that would occupy him for the next twelve years. In 1880, he was appointed to an assistant professorship in philosophy at Harvard.

John Fiske, who was the same age as James and a member of The Metaphysical Club, had become a highly regarded thinker by 1878. Four years earlier, he had published his *Outlines of Cosmic Philosophy*, thereby establishing his reputation for having the ability to speak on broad cultural issues. Fiske helped popularize Darwin's theory of evolution and was a disciple of Herbert Spencer's evolutionary philosophy. According to Henry Steele Commager, it was Fiske who "made the findings of Darwin respectable even to the clergy and, in impersonal alliance with William Graham Sumner, conquered America for the doctrines of Spencer."[18]

Nine years before the publication of *Origin of Species*, Spencer had published a book advocating a theory of evolution similar to Darwin's (but with a strong Lamarckian bent). When Darwin's work was published,

> Spencer became so enthusiastic about it that he decided to write a series of volumes which would apply the conception of evolution to all the sciences. In this way he hoped to develop an all-inclusive philosophical theory, a synthetic philosophy, as he called it, which would incorporate all scientific data and use a scientific methodology. From 1860 to 1893 Spencer worked on this project, producing volumes on metaphysics, biology, psychology, sociology, and ethics. In spite of occasional inaccuracies about scientific details, Spencer's work obtained world recognition.[19]

Spencer's influence on American thought in the second half of the nineteenth century was particularly strong. He formulated his laissez-faire philosophy in such a way that it appealed "at once to the traditional individualism and the acquisitive instincts of Americans, who were able without too great inconsistency to regard whatever they did, individually, as in harmony with evolution and whatever government or society did, collectively, as contrary to natural law."[20] At least within America it appeared that Spencer might realize his dream of completing the great work of Darwin by bringing human society within the embrace of the theory of evolution.

The problem that Spencer and Fiske set out to solve was a formidable one. The most thoughtful men in America in the decades following the Civil War were gravely troubled by "the problem of the sanctions behind those moral and religious teachings which for centuries had guided the footsteps of men along paths of righteousness to salvation."[21] As interpreted by Fiske, the evolutionary philosophies of Darwin and Spencer seem to solve that problem:

> Although at first they seemed to threaten the very foundations of traditional belief, a more mature appreciation of their meaning—Fiske's, for example— discovered that the substitution of evolution for the Scriptures or for Reason derogated neither from the sovereignty of the Supreme Lawgiver nor from the majesty of the laws. The doctrines of evolution certified a universe governed by Law and the progressive destiny of Man, not on the basis of fallible Reason nor on mere intuition but by the irreproachable findings of science. Evolution outmoded rather than nullified the Enlightenment and Transcendentalism, for though its methods were profoundly different, its conclusions were much the same. Progress was no longer a mere conclusion of logic but a necessity of nature. Scientific determinism lost its terrors when it was seen to be benevolent, shaping Nature and Man for ends that could justly be called divine. Where the Enlightenment had built a Heavenly City and Transcendentalism a Utopia, evolution held out the dazzling prospect of a future more glorious than anything that either had imagined, and its promise carried conviction. Morality itself was furnished, for the first time, with a scientific foundation. Reason and intuition had wrestled vainly with the problem of evil in a universe logically or ideally good; evolution made the problem irrelevant, for evil, which was now seen to be but a maladjustment to nature, was destined inevitably to disappear in the larger harmony which was good.[22]

It seemed that post–Civil War America had finally found a philosophy it could live with.

Even William James, when he first read Spencer at the age of eighteen, was "carried away with enthusiasm by the intellectual perspective which it seemed to open,"[23] and he confessed that a few years later, when he heard his friend, Charles Peirce, attack Spencer, he felt "spiritually wounded, as by the defacement of a sacred image."[24] But James soon shared Peirce's point of view. For even though Spencer's evolutionary philosophy promised ultimate perfection, it was not a perfection to which individual men could make individual contributions. "Though it seemed at first glance far from exacting in its demands, it imposed in the end a price higher than that required even by Calvinism—the logical abandonment of free will,"[25] and James would have none of that. "Was a philosophy which presented a closed universe, its mechanics patented by Herbert Spencer, its distant promises underwritten by John Fiske, consistent with the American character, adaptable to the American tradition?"[26] James thought not.

But he had to focus his criticism. "My quarrel with Spencer," he wrote in 1878, "is not that he makes much of environment, but that he makes nothing of the glaring and patent fact of subjective interests which cooperate with the environment in moulding intelligence. These interests form a true spontaneity and justify the refusal of *a priori* schools to admit that mind was pure, passive receptivity."[27] In "Remarks on Spencer's Definition of Mind," James develops the thesis that the central fact of mind is interest or preference, the germinal idea of his psychology, epistemology, and philosophy of religion.

CHAPTER THREE

Peircean Pragmatism

In 1868, Peirce had held that the question of whether to define belief as that judgment that is accompanied by a feeling of conviction or as that judgment from which a man will act is "a mere question of words."[1] Peirce no longer believed this in 1878. What changed his mind was being introduced to the views of Alexander Bain in meetings of The Metaphysical Club, which Peirce and James had founded in 1871. Years later, Peirce described the situation:

> It was in the earliest seventies that a knot of us young men in Old Cambridge, calling ourselves, half-ironically, half-defiantly, "The Metaphysical Club,"—for agnosticism was then riding its high horse, and was frowning superbly upon all metaphysics—used to meet, sometimes in my study, sometimes in that of William James. It may be that some of our old-time confederates would today not care to have such wild-oats-sowings made public, though there was nothing but boiled oats, milk, and sugar in the mess. Mr. Justice Holmes, however, will not, I believe, take it ill that we are proud to remember his membership; nor will Joseph Warner, Esq. Nicholas St. John Green was one of the most interested fellows, a skillful lawyer and a learned one, a disciple of Jeremy Bentham. His extraordinary power of disrobing warm and breathing truth of the draperies of long worn formulas was what attracted attention to him everywhere. In particular, he often urged the importance of applying Bain's definition of belief, as "that upon which a man is prepared to act." From this definition, pragmatism is scarce more than a corollary; so that I am disposed to think of him as the grandfather of pragmatism.[2]

What interested Peirce and the others was Nicholas St. John Green's "extraordinary power of disrobing warm and breathing truth of the draperies of long worn formulas." For warm and breathing truth is just what every pragmatist is after; and the draperies of long worn formulas are what always seemed to be hiding all but the grossest form of such truth. So, how did Nicholas St. John Green do it? Why was he the one who could always get through the hackneyed phrases and find the kernel of truth in what was being said? How would Green himself have answered these questions? Well, "he often urged the importance of applying Bain's definition of belief, as 'that upon which a man is prepared to act.' " So it seems that Green didn't think this definition of belief unimportant. It's not a mere matter of words at all—it's a matter of how one conceives the nature of thought, of a mind, of a human being.

The leading idea of Peirce's best-known essays—"The Fixation of Belief" (1877) and "How to Make Our Ideas Clear" (1878)—is that of *doubt*: doubt as a natural phenomenon, doubt as a state with which everyone is familiar. Peirce distinguished it from belief in three ways:[3]

1. There is a dissimilarity between the sensation that characteristically accompanies doubting (wishing to ask a question) and the one that characteristically accompanies coming to believe (wishing to pronounce a judgment).
2. The feeling of believing is a more or less sure indication of there being established in our nature some habit which will determine our actions. Doubt never has such an effect.
3. Doubt is an uneasy and dissatisfied state from which we struggle to free ourselves and pass into the state of belief; while the latter is a calm and satisfactory state which we do not wish to avoid or to change into a belief in anything else.

The last point is particularly important. Doubt is an uneasy, irritating, dissatisfied state. It provides no guide for action, no way of proceeding. So we struggle to free ourselves from it, to acquire a habit of action, to attain a state of belief. Peirce calls this struggle to turn doubt into belief (or disbelief) *inquiry* ("though it must be admitted that this is sometimes not a very apt designation"[4]).

He maintains that the irritation of doubt is the only immediate motive for the struggle to attain belief and the fixation of belief (the settlement of opinion) is the sole object of inquiry:

> The irritation of doubt is the only immediate motive for the struggle to attain belief. It is certainly best for us that our beliefs should be such as may truly guide our actions so as to satisfy our desires; and this reflection will make us reject every belief which does not seem to have been so formed as to insure this result. But it will only do so by creating a doubt in the place of that belief. With the doubt, therefore, the struggle begins, and with the cessation of doubt it ends. Hence, the sole object of inquiry is the settlement of opinion. We may fancy that this is not enough for us, and that we seek, not merely an opinion, but a true opinion. But put

this fancy to the test, and it proves groundless; for as soon as a firm belief is reached we are entirely satisfied, whether the belief be true or false. And it is clear that nothing out of the sphere of our knowledge can be our object, for nothing which does not affect the mind can be the motive for mental effort. The most that can be maintained is, that we seek for a belief that we shall *think* to be true. But we think each one of our beliefs to be true, and, indeed, it is mere tautology to say so.[5]

Given that thought itself is being construed as inquiry and that the fixation of belief is the only purpose of inquiry, one begins to see the important role that belief (in Bain's sense) plays in pragmatism: "The production of belief is the sole function of thought," Peirce said, and both James and Dewey would concur with this judgment. Further,

The action of thought is excited by the initiation of doubt, and ceases when belief is attained; so that the production of belief is the sole function of thought. All these words, however, are too strong for my purpose. It is as if I had described the phenomena as they appear under a mental microscope. Doubt and Belief, as the words are commonly employed, relate to religious or other grave discussions. But here I use them to designate the starting of any question, no matter how small or how great, and the resolution of it. If, for instance, in a horse-car, I pull out my purse and find a five-cent nickel and five coppers, I decide, while my hand is going to the purse, in which way I will pay my fare. To call such a question Doubt, and my decision Belief, is certainly to use words very disproportionate to the occasion. To speak of such a doubt as causing an irritation which needs to be appeased, suggests a temper which is uncomfortable to the verge of insanity. Yet, looking at the matter minutely, it must be admitted that, if there is the least hesitation as to whether I shall pay the five coppers or the nickel (as there will be sure to be, unless I act from some previously contracted habit in the matter), though irritation is too strong a word, yet I am excited to such small mental activity as may be necessary to deciding how I shall act.[6]

Thus, in interpreting thought as inquiry, as the activity of appeasing doubt by producing belief, Peirce realizes that he is using all three terms in somewhat extended senses. He is using 'doubt' and 'belief' to designate "the starting of any question, no matter how small or how great, and the resolution of it"; and he means by 'inquiry' no more than that transition from question to resolution.

Doubt generally arises from some indecision, however momentary, in our actions. We aren't sure whether to use the nickel or the five pennies. We don't know whether a real or a fictitious event is being described. We are ready to neither agree nor disagree. This creates stress. For example, it has been shown that laboratory rats develop so-called executive ulcers if they have to cross an electric grid that shocks their feet in order to obtain food or water.[7] It isn't the electric shocks that cause the ulcers; it is the stress brought about by the indecision of whether to cross the grid or not. Again, when two monkeys are placed in harnesses in such a way that one of them can press a bar at least once every twenty seconds to avoid a periodic shock to both monkeys' feet, the decision-making monkey, but not the other one, will have ulcers within three or four weeks.[8] Thus to appease doubt is to eliminate stress. And it is the doubt itself that stimulates one to do so. Doubt

> stimulates the mind to an activity which may be slight or energetic, calm or turbulent. Images pass rapidly through consciousness, one incessantly melting into another, until at last, when all is over—it may be a fraction of a second, in an hour, or after long years—we find ourselves decided as to how we should act under such circumstances as those which occasioned our hesitation. In other words, we have attained belief.[9]

So Peirce sees thought as a series of mental acts. They have beginnings, middles, and ends. They result in systems of relationships in the succession of sensations that flow through the mind. Peirce notes that various systems of relationship of succession can subsist together between the same sensations:

> These different systems are distinguished by having different motives, ideas, or functions. Thought is only one such system, for its sole motive, idea, and function is to produce belief, and whatever does not concern that purpose belongs to some other system of relations. The action of thinking may incidently have other results; it may serve to amuse us, for example, and among *dilettanti* it is not rare to find those who have so perverted thought to the purpose of pleasure that it seems to vex them to think that the questions upon which they delight to exercise it may ever get finally settled; and a positive discovery which takes a favourite subject out of the arena of literary debate is met with ill-concealed dislike. This disposition is the very debauchery of thought.[10]

It is what, one presumes, Nicholas St. John Green was so clever at exposing. It is what Peirce, in writing "How to Make Our Ideas Clear," is set on opposing. He believes we need a way of distinguishing the thought itself from other elements that may accompany it. It is to this end that he urges us to bear in mind that thought itself can never be made to aim at anything but the settlement of opinion, the production of belief. "Thought in action has for its only possible motive the attainment of thought at rest; and whatever does not refer to belief is no part of the thought itself."[11]

This is why it is so important to be clear about the nature of belief. Peirce notes that it has just three properties:[12]

1. It is something that we are aware of.
2. It appeases the irritation of doubt.
3. It involves the establishment in our nature of a rule of action, a habit.

Since belief appeases the irritation of doubt, which is the sole motive for thinking, thought comes to rest, at least momentarily, when belief is reached. But it does not remain at rest for long—since belief is a rule of action, its life is in its application, and each application can open the door to further doubt and, therefore, further thought to appease it. Peirce sees thought as "a thread of melody running through the succession of our sensations."[13] And belief, according to Peirce, "is the demi-cadence which closes a musical phrase in the symphony of our intellectual life."[14]

What Bain's definition of 'belief' provided for Peirce's pragmatic analysis of thought was a *principle of individuation:*

> The essence of belief is the establishment of a habit; and different beliefs are distinguished by the different modes of action to which they give rise. If beliefs do not differ in this respect, if they appease the same doubt by producing the same rule of action, then no mere differences in the manner of consciousness of them can make them different beliefs, any more than playing a tune in different keys is playing different tunes.[15]

We have here two of the fundamental principles of Peirce's pragmatism. The first goes back to Bain:

1. Beliefs are identical if and only if they give rise to the same habit of action.

The second is original with Peirce:

2. Beliefs give rise to the same habit of action if and only if they appease the same doubt by producing the same rule of action.

Notice, in particular, that according to this *pragmatic* account of belief, the question of whether my belief that Peirce decided to use the pennies is the same as my belief that Peirce decided to save the nickel *has nothing whatsoever to do with* the question of whether the sentences 'Peirce decided to use the pennies' and 'Peirce decided to save the nickel' are synonymous. Antonymous sentences can be used to express the same belief and synonymous sentences (if there are any) can be used to express different beliefs.

If we keep principles 1 and 2 in mind, we will keep it in mind that "the whole function of thought is to produce habits of action" and that "whatever there is connected with a thought, but irrelevant to its purpose, is an accretion to it, but no part of it."[16] Therefore, to develop the meaning of a thought, we need only determine what habit of action it produces, for what a thought means is simply a matter of what habits it involves:

> Now, the identity of a habit depends on how it might lead us to act, not merely under such circumstances as are likely to arise, but under such as might possibly occur, no matter how improbable they may be. What the habit is depends on *when* and *how* it causes us to act. As for the *when*, every stimulus to action is derived from perception; as for the *how*, every purpose of action is to produce some sensible result. Thus, we come down to what is tangible and conceivably practical, as the root of every real distinction of thought, no matter how subtle it may be; and there is no distinction of meaning so fine as to consist in anything but a possible difference in practice.[17]

Three new pragmatic principles surface here:

3. The meaning of a thought is the belief it produces.
4. Beliefs produce the same rule of action only if they lead us to act in the same sensible situations.
5. Beliefs produce the same rule of action only if they lead us to the same sensible results.

Thus, Peirce says, we come down to what is tangible and conceivably practical—sensible situations and sensible results—at the root of every real distinction of thought, no matter how subtle it may be; and we thus arrive at a sixth principle of Peircean pragmatism:

6. There is no distinction of meaning so fine as to consist in anything but a possible difference in what is tangible and conceivably practical.

It is utterly impossible, Peirce contends, "that we should have an idea in our minds which relates to anything but conceived sensible effects of things,"[18] anything but sensible situations and sensible results. Therefore, Peirce concludes,

7. Our idea of anything *is* our idea of its sensible effects,

"and if we fancy that we have any other we deceive ourselves, and mistake a mere sensation accompanying the thought for a part of the thought itself."[19] Principle 7 plays a very important role in the development of Peirce's thought; it sets the stage for his most famous principle, the one that has come to be called the *pragmatic maxim*:

> 8. Consider what effects, that might conceivably have practical bearings, we conceive the object of our conception to have. Then our conception of these effects is the whole of our conception of the object.[20]

Let us make sure that we clearly apprehend this rule for attaining clarity of apprehension. It speaks of "the object of our conception." As his examples show, Peirce is thinking of properties (hardness, weight, force, reality, . . .). Take hardness, for example, and apply the maxim to it:

> Consider what effects, that might conceivably have practical bearings, we conceive hardness to have. Then our conception of these effects is the whole of our conception of hardness.

How do we consider what effects, which might conceivably have practical bearings, we conceive hardness to have? *By asking ourselves what we mean by calling a thing hard.* (At least that's what Peirce actually does.) And we should ask what we mean by calling a thing hard "not merely under such circumstances as are likely to arise, but under such as might possibly occur, no matter how improbable they may be."[21] Unfortunately, Peirce does not do that himself. He considers only one circumstance, one in which the thing being called hard is, perhaps, a diamond or other stone, and so he comes up with just one "effect":

(E$_1$) It will not be scratched by many other substances.

Let us consider some further circumstances and further "sensible effects." If the subject of which hardness is being predicated is not a stone but a chair, a quite different effect will be predicted:

(E$_2$) Not many people will sit in it comfortably for very long.

If the subject is neither a stone nor a chair but a question, then

(E$_3$)   Not many of those to whom it is addressed will be able to answer it correctly

is the sensible effect. When the subject is a knot, the effect we intend is

(E$_4$)   Not many people will be able to untie it in a brief period of time;

and

(E$_5$)   Not many people will be able to solve it in a brief period of time

is the effect that might conceivably have practical bearings when the thing being called hard is a *problem*. In the case of a hard worker, we have this effect:

(E$_6$)   Not many of his co-workers will outwork him;

and we have this effect,

(E$_7$)   Not many rains will deposit as much water in as short a time

when we are speaking of a hard rain. And so on for a hard task, a hard fall, a piece of hard luck, a hard treatment, a hard look, a hard winter, a hard feeling, etc. In each case, there is some sensible effect, some effect that might have practical bearings, some effect that can serve as a *criterion* of whether or not the thing in question can truly be said to be hard. And since our idea of hardness is our idea of the sensible effects E$_1$, E$_2$, E$_3$, . . . of hardness, once we have considered what sensible effects we conceive hardness to have, our conception of these sensible effects is the whole of our conception of hardness.

Thus we can reformulate the pragmatic maxim. Let P be any monadic predicate that expresses a property that we are trying to get clear about. Peirce's maxim can then be given this alternative formulation:

8a. Ask what are our criteria for calling a thing P. Then our conception of those criteria is the whole of our conception of P-ness (P-ity, P-hood, . . .).

We shall take 8a as our official version of "the pragmatic maxim." What it crisply formulates, however, is not so much Peirce's pragmatism as his *experimentalism*. Years later, he would remark that he had

> been led by much experience to believe that every physicist, and every chemist, and, in short, every master in any department of experimental science, has had his mind moulded by his life in the laboratory to a degree that is little suspected. The experimentalist himself can hardly be fully aware of it, for the reason that the men whose intellects he really knows about are much like himself in this respect. With intellects of widely different training from his own, whose education has largely been a thing learned out of books, he will never become inwardly intimate, be he on ever so familiar terms with them; for he and they are as oil and water, and though they be shaken up together, it is remarkable how quickly they will go their several mental ways, without having gained more than a faint flavour from the association. Were those other men only to take skillful soundings of the experimentalist's mind—which is just what they are unqualified to do, for the most part—they would soon discover that, excepting perhaps upon topics where his mind is trammelled by personal feeling or by his bringing up, his disposition is to think of everything just as everything is thought of in the laboratory, that is, as a question of experimentation . . . you will find that whatever assertion you may make to him, he will either understand as meaning that if a given prescription for an experiment ever can be and ever is carried out in act, an experience of a given description will result, or else he will see no sense at all in what you say.[22]

Each of Peirce's "effects, that might conceivably have practical bearings," each of our *criteria*, gives (somewhat vaguely) a "prescription for an experiment" and predicts that if it "ever is carried out in act, an experience of a given description will result." For instance, E_7 is our criterion for a hard rain. What experiment does it prescribe? It prescribes finding out what the rate of this rainfall is and comparing to it, say, the ten greatest rates of rainfall over the past ten years. And what result does it predict? It predicts that this rainfall will be near the head of the list. To develop the habit of filtering assertions through the pragmatic maxim is to develop the experimentalistic habit of mind, that is, the "disposition . . . to think of everything just as everything is thought of in the laboratory, that is, as a question of experimentation."

Clearly, Peirce put great stock in the experimental method, the method of science. In "The Fixation of Belief," he surveys the methods of fixing belief that have been tried. What Peirce calls the *method of tenacity* only fixes belief in the individual, whereas the real problem is "how to fix belief, not in the individual merely, but in the community." Two of the other three methods, the *method of authority* and the *a priori method*, do serve to settle opinion in the community, but they cannot claim to do so objectively, that is, in terms of what is entirely independent of what you or I or anyone thinks. To objectively fix belief in the community,

> it is necessary that a method should be found by which our beliefs may be determined by nothing human, but by some external permanency— by something upon which our thinking has no effect. . . . Our external permanency would not be external, in our sense, if it was restricted in its influence to one individual. It must be something which affects, or might affect, every man. And, though these affections are necessarily as various as are individual conditions, yet the method must be such that the ultimate conclusion of every man shall be the same. Such is the method of science. Its fundamental hypothesis, restated in more familiar language, is this: There are Real things, whose characters are entirely independent of our opinions about them; those Reals affect our senses according to regular laws, and, though our sensations are as different as are our relations to the objects, yet, by taking advantage of the laws of perception, we can ascertain by reasoning how things really and truly are; and any man, if he have sufficient experience and he reason enough about it, will be led to the one True conclusion. The new conception here involved is that of Reality.[23]

In order to clearly apprehend this idea of reality, Peirce urges us to apply the pragmatic maxim. According to it, he tells us in "How to Make Our Ideas Clear,"

> reality, like every other quality, consists in the peculiar sensible effects which things partaking of it produce. The only effect which real things have is to cause belief, for all the sensations which they excite emerge into consciousness in the form of beliefs. The question therefore is, how is true belief (or belief in the real) distinguished from false belief (or belief in fiction). Now, as we have seen in the former paper, the ideas of truth and falsehood, in their full development, appertain exclusively to the experimental method of settling opinion.[24]

And he goes on to point out how the followers of this method of settling opinion

> are animated by a cheerful hope that the process of investigation, if only pushed far enough, will give one certain solution to each question to which they apply it. One man may investigate the velocity of light by studying the transits of Venus and the aberration of the stars; another by the oppositions of Mars and the eclipses of Jupiter's satellites; a third by

the method of Fizeau; a fourth by that of Foucault; a fifth by the motions of the curves of Lissajoux, a sixth, a seventh, an eighth, and a ninth, may follow the different methods of comparing the measures of statical and dynamical electricity. They may at first obtain different results, but, as each perfects his method, and processes, the results are found to move steadily together toward a destined centre. So with all scientific research. Different minds may set out with the most antagonistic views, but the progress of investigation carries them by a force outside of themselves to one and the same conclusion. This activity of thought by which we are carried, not where we wish, but to a fore-ordained goal, is like the operation of destiny. No modification of the point of view taken, no selection of other facts for study, no natural bent of mind even, can enable a man to escape the predestinate opinion. This great hope is embodied in the conception of truth and reality. The opinion which is fated to be ultimately agreed to by all who investigate, is what we mean by the truth, and the object represented in this opinion is the real. That is the way I would explain reality.[25]

Here we have two final principles of Peircean pragmatism:

9. A true belief is one which is fated to be ultimately agreed to by all who investigate scientifically.
10. Any object represented in a true belief is real.

CHAPTER FOUR

Inchoate Pragmatism

Late in life, Peirce asked James: "Who originated the term *pragmatism*, I or you? Where did it first appear in print? What do you understand by it?"[1] James answered: "You invented 'pragmatism' for which I gave you full credit in a lecture entitled 'Philosophical Conceptions and Practical Results.' "[2]

If this was intended as an answer to Peirce's second question, it is not at all clear that James is correct. In "Philosophical Conceptions and Practical Results," James only refers to "How to Make Our Ideas Clear," and the word 'pragmatism' doesn't occur in that paper. It may not have appeared in print prior to 1898! It seems clear (at least) that Peirce frequently used it as a term of art in discussions within The Metaphysical Club. But it may well be that William James introduced the term 'pragmatism'—as well as what was to become its denotation—into the philosophical literature in that lecture to G. H. Howison's Berkeley Philosophical Union in 1898.

We may call adherence to Peirce's principles 1–10 *Peircean pragmatism*, but neither Peirce nor anyone else called it that between 1878 and 1898. Moreover, virtually no one called it anything: Charles Sanders Peirce himself was a virtual unknown in the philosophical world of the 1880's and 1890's.

Still, as in his great work on psychology, the influence of Peirce and the discussions within The Metaphysical Club and among various of its members pervaded James's philosophical writings during these two decades. In 1897, James dedicated the volume entitled *The Will to Believe*: "To My Old Friend, Charles Sanders Peirce, to whose philosophic comradeship in old times and to whose writings in more recent years I owe more incitement and help than I can express or repay." And, indeed, Peirce's footprints are everywhere visible: The test of belief is willingness to act; every way of classifying a thing is but a way of handling it for some particular purpose; willingness to act as if it were true is the criterion for the life of a hypothesis; and so on. But what

is as important (or more important) for the student to see is that, as
Henry Steele Commager remarked of James:

> Even before he had come to any definition of his own philosophy, his
> philosophical preconceptions were fixed: a suspicion of all absolutes, all
> rigidities, and all systems; an inclination to leave all questions open to
> reconsideration; an indulgence of eccentricity and nonconformity; a pref-
> erence for what was artistically and emotionally as well as intellectually
> appealing; a compelling consciousness of moral obligation.[3]

In "The Sentiment of Rationality," an essay of 1879, James defines
that sentiment as "a strong feeling of ease, peace, and rest that accompanies the transition from a state of puzzle and perplexity to one of
rational comprehension. It is a feeling of sufficiency—of 'the sufficiency
of the present moment, of its absoluteness' "[4]—an absence of all need
to explain it, account for it, or justify it. "As soon, in short, as we are
enabled from any cause whatever to think with perfect fluency, the thing
we think of seems to us *pro tanto* rational."[5] It is the way we feel when
we discover what is wrong with the car, why it keeps stalling, or when
we discover a proof for a theorem whose derivation has been alluding
us. It is what we feel when we discover a philosophy—a view of the
world, a "conception of the frame of things"[6]—that *we* can accept. A
philosophy, to be acceptable to us, must not only be rational; it must
strike us as rational. Surely this is at least part of what Plato had in
mind when he urged us to think of knowledge as recollection, and it
is what Woody Guthrie had in mind when he said that he had always
wanted to be a man who told people what they already knew (but
somehow lacked words for). A philosophy that is accompanied by the
sentiment of rationality is one that strikes us as the final word on the
subject. James characterizes our attitude toward such a system of thought
by saying that we feel that it

> would bring theory down to a single point, at which every human being's
> practical life would begin. It would solve all the antinomies and contra-
> dictions, it would let loose all the right impulses and emotions; and
> everyone, on hearing it, would say, "Why, that *is* the truth!—*that* is what
> I have been believing, that is what I have really been living on all this
> time, but I never could find the words for it before. All that eludes, all
> that flickers and twinkles, all that invites and vanishes even whilst inviting,
> is here made a solidity and a possession. Here is the end of unsatisfactoriness,
> here the beginning of unimpeded clearness, joy, and power."[7]

No philosophical system that fails to wake this sentiment will become
a philosophy by which men live their lives.

To wake the sentiment of rationality, a philosophy must satisfy two basic types of human needs: those we have in virtue of the fact that we have a need to know, our "theoretic needs," and those we have in virtue of the fact that we have a need to act, our "practical needs." Preeminent among our theoretic needs are "the passion for simplification" and "the passion for distinguishing." According to James, "a man's philosophic attitude is determined by the balance in him of these two cravings."[8] Our most important practical needs are the need, in a general way at least, "to banish uncertainty from the future";[9] and the need "to define the future congruously with our spontaneous powers":[10] "If we survey the field of history and ask what future all great periods of revival, of expansion of the human mind, display in common, we shall find, I think, simply this: that each and all of them have said to the human being, 'The inmost nature of the reality is congenial to *powers* which you possess.' "[11]

Any philosophy, or any conception of the world, in order to be accepted by living, breathing human beings, must come to terms with these needs, that is, the ones that define us as knowing and acting animals. The point to note here, and it is a basic principle of James's philosophy, is that the conditions of acceptability of a philosophy are just as important (perhaps even more important) as its truth conditions. James's point is that, in the last analysis, it is always our nature—human nature—not the nature of reality in general, which must decide what we are to think about the nature of reality in general. So, philosophies that do not satisfy these human demands, that do not wake the sentiment of rationality, will not be accepted; and, hence, the question of their truth or falsity will be beside the point.

The *dilemma of determinism* is that it

leads us to call our judgments of regret wrong, because they are pessimistic in implying that what is impossible yet ought to be. But how then about the judgments of regret themselves? If they are wrong, other judgments, judgments of approval presumably, ought to be in their place. But, as they are necessitated, nothing else *can* be in their place; and the universe is just what it was before,—namely, a place in which what ought to be appears impossible. We have got one foot out of the pessimistic bag, but the other one sinks all the deeper. We have rescued our actions from the bonds of evil, but our judgments are now held fast. When murders and treacheries cease to be sins, regrets are errors. The theoretic and the active life thus play a kind of see-saw with each other on the ground of evil. The rise of either sends the other down. Murder and treachery can't be good without regret being bad: regret can't be good without treachery and murder being bad. Both, however, are supposed to have been fore-doomed, so *something* must be bad in the world. It must be a place of which either sin or error forms a necessary part. From this dilemma there seems at first sight no escape. Are we then so soon to fall back into the pessimism from which we thought we had emerged?[12]

We have noted previously that, for James, the problem of free will or determinism was not a purely academic matter. Since the facts themselves can neither prove nor disprove determinism, one is entitled to take into account the grave practical issues that are at stake. Determinism, which denies that anything could be different than it actually is makes absolutely impossible what our human nature makes us believe ought to be the case. Such a philosophy can never evoke the sentiment of rationality.

It is interesting to contrast this essay with Peirce's "The Doctrine of Necessity Examined" of 1892. Peirce believes that he had "subjected to fair examination all the important reasons for adhering to the theory of universal necessity [determinism], and [had] shown their nullity."[13] The contrast is not between Peircean pragmatism and Jamesian pragmatism, but between Peircean experimentalism and Jamesian humanism. The congruence of their conclusions is also impressive.

"The Moral Philosopher and the Moral Life" is the only paper on ethical theory that William James ever published. "The main purpose of this paper," he tells us, "is to show that there is no such thing possible as an ethical philosophy dogmatically made up in advance. We all help to determine the content of ethical philosophy so far as we contribute to the race's moral life. In other words, there can be no final truth in ethics any more than in physics, until the last man has had his experience and said his say."[14] James's point is that there is no such thing as morality in the nature of things: For there to be morality, there must be humanity. "Nothing can be good or right except so far as some consciousness feels it to be good or thinks it to be right."[15] And there will no doubt be some other consciousness that feels something incompatible to be good or thinks an opposing action to be right; who is to decide between them?

Since everything which is demanded is by that fact a good, must not the guiding principle for ethical philosophy (since all demands conjointly cannot be satisfied in this poor world) be simply to satisfy at all times *as many demands as we can*? That act must be the best act, accordingly, which makes for the *best whole,* in the sense of awakening the least sum of dissatisfactions. In the casuistic scale, therefore, those ideals must be written highest which *prevail at the least cost,* or by whose realization the least possible number of other ideals are destroyed. . . . The course of history is nothing but the story of men's struggles from generation to generation to find the more and more inclusive order. *Invent some manner* of realizing your own ideals which will also satisfy the alien demands,— that and that only is the path of peace! Following this path, society has shaken itself into one sort of relative equilibrium after another by a series of social discoveries quite analogous to those of science.[16]

We see here the beginnings of a theme in pragmatic thought that will be developed with great finesse by John Dewey. As James writes, "so far as the casuistic question goes, ethical science is just like physical science."[17]

"The Will to Believe," James wrote to F. H. Bradley, is a "luckless title, which should have been 'Right to Believe.' "[18] Surely he was right. To mistitle one's most widely read essay, and to do so in such a way as to suggest exactly the misunderstanding that the critics most delight in, is certainly a cause for regret. The theme of this essay is that human beings sometimes have a right to adopt a believing attitude even when the available evidence is insufficient to justify belief. This was written in direct opposition to such positivists as W. K. Clifford who contend that to believe in such a circumstance is to act "in defiance of our duty to mankind."[19] There is no ambiguity in Clifford's position: "It is wrong always, everywhere, and for every one, to believe anything upon insufficient evidence."[20]

To counter this extraordinary claim, James needed only to assert a very limited thesis, *viz.* that it is right sometimes, somewhere, and for someone to believe something upon insufficient evidence. This hardly seems controversial. "Our belief in truth itself, for instance, that there is a truth, and that our minds and it are made for each other,—what is it but a passionate affirmation of desire, in which our social system backs us up?"[21]

Nonetheless, because of James's luckless title and his eagerness to apply his carefully limited thesis ("Our passional nature not only lawfully may, but must, decide an opinion between propositions, whenever it is a genuine option that cannot by its nature be decided on intellectual grounds; for to say, under such circumstances, 'Do not decide, but leave the question open,' is itself a passional decision—just like deciding yes or no,—and is attended with the same risk of losing the truth."[22]) to religious issues, many of which are not obviously genuine options (i.e., forced, living, and momentous options), this essay is frequently castigated as a defense of wishful thinking. But that is a ludicrous interpretation. Ralph Barton Perry, it seems to me, gives just the right summation. Speaking of James, he said:

He was accused of encouraging *willfulness* or *wantonness* of belief, or of advocating belief for belief's sake, whereas his whole purpose had been to *justify* belief. He had affirmed that belief was voluntary, but had naturally assumed that, in this as in other cases, volition would be governed by motives and illuminated by reasons. His critics had accused him of advocating *license* in belief, whereas, on the contrary, his aim had been to formulate rules for belief. And whatever one might think of its extensive religious applications, the thesis had been simple. He had argued that in certain cases where both belief and doubt are possible there is a greater likelihood of getting the truth by believing than by doubting—or at least an equal likelihood, with other advantages besides. Over and above the risk of incurring error, to which science is so acutely alive, there is another risk to be considered, the risk, namely, of losing truth.[23]

Of the six lawyers in The Metaphysical Club, Oliver Wendell Holmes, Jr., followed the path of the law the farthest, all the way to the United States Supreme Court, on which he sat for thirty years. In *The Common Law*, which Holmes published in 1882, he maintains that "the life of the law has not been logic, it has been experience. The felt necessities of the time, the prevalent moral and political theories, intuitions of public policy, avowed or unconscious, even the prejudices which judges share with their fellow men, have a good deal more to do than the syllogism in determining the rules by which men shall be governed."[24]

It was while he was an active participant in The Metaphysical Club that Holmes formulated his "prediction theory of law." What are lawyers paid to do? To accurately predict what the courts will in fact do, and nothing more pretentious. As Holmes said in a famous essay called "The Path of the Law," the object of the study of law is "prediction, the prediction of the incidence of the [use of] public force through the instrumentality of the courts."[25] Furthermore, Holmes's years of service on the bench, as well as his down-to-earth theorizing about the nature of law, show the influence of pragmatism. The United States Constitution, he held, "is an experiment, as all life is an experiment."[26] That was why he was always willing to strike down as unconstitutional all invasions of basic civil liberties. Because without them, both social and personal experimentation becomes impossible.

CHAPTER FIVE

Jamesian Pragmatism

James's "Philosophical Conceptions and Practical Results" is the lecture in which pragmatism was announced to the philosophical community and, presumably, it was where the term 'pragmatism' was introduced into the philosophical literature. His *Pragmatism* (1907) is the book that spread pragmatism around the world. In 1908, John Dewey wrote of that book that

> it is in any case beyond a critic's praise or blame. It is more likely to take place as a philosophical classic than any other writing of our day. A critic who should attempt to appraise it would probably give one more illustration of the sterility of criticism compared with the productiveness of creative genius. Even those who dislike pragmatism can hardly fail to find much of profit in the exhibition of Mr. James' instinct for concrete facts, the breadth of his sympathies, and his illuminating insights. Unreserved frankness, lucid imagination, varied contacts with life digested into summary and trenchant conclusions, keen perceptions of human nature in the concrete, a constant sense of the subordination of philosophy to life, capacity to put things into an English which projects ideas as if bodily into space till they are solid things to walk around and survey from different sides—these things are not so common in philosophy that they may not smell sweet even by the name of pragmatism.[1]

For the reasons Dewey so eloquently stated, I make no apology for basing an account of James's own brand of pragmatism on that book, which "was never meant for a treatise, but for a sketch,"[2] a book that was only written "to *win a platform* for more accurate discussion."[3]

But, for both historical and pedagogical reasons, we begin with James's paper on "Philosophical Conceptions and Practical Results." There he credits Peirce with "the principle of practicalism—or pragmatism, as he called it, when I first heard him enunciate it at Cambridge in the early '70's."[4] In 1898, James thought that 'practicalism' was at least as good a term as 'pragmatism' for the doctrine Peirce introduced, presumably because the latter term "is derived from the same Greek word *pragma*, meaning action, from which our words 'practice' and 'practical' come."[5] At least that is what he said in 1907, no doubt responding to the following passage from a paper ("What Pragmatism Is") Peirce published in *The Monist* in 1905. Peirce speaks of his (youthful) self in the third person:

> That laboratory life did not prevent the writer (who here and in what follows simply exemplifies the experimentalist type) from becoming interested in methods of thinking; . . . Endeavouring, as a man of that type naturally would, to formulate what he so approved, he framed the theory that a *conception*, that is, the rational purport of a word or other expression, lies exclusively in its conceivable bearing upon the conduct of life; so that, since obviously nothing that might not result from experiment can have any direct bearing upon conduct, if one can define accurately all the conceivable experimental phenomena which the affirmation or denial of a concept could imply, one will have therein a complete definition of the concept, and *there is absolutely nothing more in it*. For this doctrine he invented the name *pragmatism*. Some of his friends wished him to call it *practicism* or *practicalism* (perhaps on the ground that *praktikos* is better Greek than *pragmatikos*). But for one who learned philosophy out of Kant, as the writer, . . . had done, and who still thought in Kantian terms most readily, *praktisch* and *pragmatisch* were as far apart as the two poles, the former belonging to a region of thought where no mind of the experimentalist type can ever make sure of solid ground under his feet, the latter expressing relation to some definite human purpose. Now quite the most striking feature of the new theory was its recognition of an inseparable connection between rational cognition and rational purpose; and that consideration it was which determined the preference for the name *pragmatism*.[6]

So, far from regarding the two terms as synonyms, Peirce thinks of 'pragmatism' as being in sharp contrast to 'practicalism.' For he was thinking in Kantian terms, and Kant had established a distinction between what is practical and what is pragmatic. For Kant, it is moral laws that are practical. Hence, since he held such laws to be *a priori*, what is practical in Kantian terms belongs to a region of thought (the *a priori*) "where no mind of the experimental type can ever make sure of solid ground under his feet." On the other hand, Kant held that rules of art and technique are pragmatic. (These, of course, are *a posteriori*: They are based on experience.) So what is pragmatic in Kantian terms is that which expresses a "relation to some definite human purpose": a rule is a rule *for* accomplishing some purpose. And that is what caught Peirce's attention. Since "quite the most striking feature of [his] new theory was its recognition of an inseparable connection between rational cognition and rational purpose," 'pragmatism' seemed just the right coinage.

As we have formerly argued, Peirce uses this term to denote the doctrine that "if one can define accurately all the conceivable experimental phenomena which the affirmation or denial of a concept could imply, one will have therein a complete definition of the concept, and *there is absolutely nothing more in it.*"[7] We illustrated this doctrine in application to the concept of hardness. Since a concept is "the rational purport of a word or other expression," Peirce's pragmatism implies:

> If one can define accurately all the conceivable experimental phenomena which the affirmation or denial of the rational purport of hardness could imply, one will have therein a complete definition of the rational purport of hardness.

Of course we did not succeed in defining—even inaccurately—*all* the *conceivable* experimental phenomena which the predication of hardness could imply. We only (inaccurately) defined seven "conceivable experimental phenomena," or seven "effects that might conceivably have practical bearings." But if we had defined all the criteria of hardness, then we would have had therein a complete definition of the rational purport of hardness. Each of those criteria governs a particular use (to characterize a chair, a question, a worker, etc.) to which the predicate 'hard' can be put, a particular rational purpose to which the rational purport of hardness can be put. "Now quite the most striking feature of the new theory was its recognition of an inseparable connection between rational cognition and rational purpose," between meaning and use. So if one can define accurately all the criteria governing uses to which the predicate 'hard' could be put, one will have therein a complete definition of the meaning of hardness. More generally: If one can define accurately all the criteria governing uses to which a predicate can be put, one will have therein a complete definition of the meaning of what it predicates. *This* is the principle of Peirce, the principle of pragmatism.

Let us see whether this is how James understood that principle (in 1898). He set out to describe Peirce's introduction of it in "How to Make Our Ideas Clear":

> The soul and meaning of thought, [Peirce] says, can never be made to direct itself towards anything but the production of belief, belief being the demicadence which closes a musical phrase in the symphony of our intellectual life. Thought in movement has thus for its only possible motive the attainment of thought at rest. But when our thought about an object has found its rest in belief, then our action on the subject can firmly and

safely begin. Beliefs, in short, are really rules for action; and the whole function of thinking is but one step in the production of habits of action. If there were any part of a thought that made no difference in the thought's practical consequences, then that part would be no proper element of the thought's significance.[8]

James certainly begins in the right place, *viz.* with Peirce's conception of thought in action as inquiry, and thought at rest as belief. According to this conception, the only possible motive for thought in action is the attainment of belief. Of course, this is all said by James with approval. Suppose, then, that we were to ask James *why* we should want to attain belief. How would he answer? I think that he would say that, since a person's beliefs about hardness, for example, are rules governing activities with the term 'hard' that have become habits of action for that person, when *we* have acquired these habits—when *our* thought about hardness has found its rest in belief—then *our* actions with hard things "can firmly and safely begin." And what is true of hardness is true of more philosophically interesting attributes, such as goodness and reality: When our thoughts about goodness and reality have found their rest in belief, our actions with good things and real things can firmly and safely begin. James's point is that *belief exists for the sake of action.* It allows us to act with conviction and it allows us to act in safety.

It is not at all clear to me what James means by 'safety.' What do our beliefs about hardness keep us safe from? Hard luck? Hard looks? Hard winters? Hard rock? But there is a more basic problem here. James speaks in these terms: "our actions on the subject," "rules for action," "habits of action," and "the thought's practical consequences." What does he have in mind? The examples he uses help us to see. After agreeing with Peirce that only those features of a thought that make a difference in its practical consequences are to be regarded as elements of that thought's significance, James continues:

Thus the same thought may be clad in different words; but if the different words suggest no different conduct, they are mere outer accretions, and have no part in the thought's meaning. If, however, they determine conduct differently, they are essential elements of the significance. "Please open the door," and "*Veuillez ouvrir la porte*," in French, mean just the same thing; but "Damn you, open the door," although in English, *means* something very different. Thus to develop a thought's meaning we need only determine what conduct it is fitted to produce; that conduct is for us its sole significance. And the tangible fact at the root of all our thought-distinctions, however subtle, is that there is no one of them so fine as to consist in anything but a possible difference of practice.[9]

When Peirce illustrates his doctrine with examples, he uses attributes: hardness, weight, force, and reality. James is on an entirely different wave length. His examples are sentences in the imperative mood:

1. Please open the door.
2. *Veuillez ouvrir la porte.*
3. Damn you, open the door.

He says that 1 and 2 mean just the same thing, whereas 3 means something very different from either 1 or 2. The idea is that the rules— the pragmatic rules, in Kant's sense—governing the use of 1 and 2 are essentially the same. For example,

(P₁)   If someone were to say "Please open the door" to me, I would try to accommodate him;

and

(P₂)   If someone were to say *"Veuillez ouvrir la porte"* to me, I would try to accommodate him

differ only in "the outer accretion" that is quoted. That is to say, they are rules of the same form, rules of accommodation:

(Pₐ)   If someone were to say x to me, I would try to accommodate him.

On the other hand, James's pragmatic rule for 3—

(P₃)   If someone were to say "Damn you, open the door" to me, I would refuse to accommodate him

—is a rule of a quite different form, a rule of refusal:

(P_R)   If someone were to say x to me, I would refuse to accommodate him.

Instances of (P_R) differ from those of (Pₐ) in an essential way: "They determine conduct differently."

Of course, there are pragmatic rules governing the use of sentences in moods other than the imperative. James had rules of action for

4. Is the door open?

and

    5. The door is open.

as well as

    6. Open the door.

For example, James surely had a rule of form (P_A) among those governing his use of sentence 4. And he surely had pragmatic rules for these declaratives:

    7. She has a hard look.
    8. He is hard up.
    9. We had a very hard winter,

But perhaps not for these:

    10. *A Clockwork Orange* is hard reading.
    11. The free safety is a hard hitter.
    12. They only listen to hard rock.

Among James's rules for 7, 8, and 9, let us conjecture, are these:

(P_4) If someone were to say "She has a hard look" to me, I should take them to be suggesting that her look is indicative of her past.

(P_5) If someone were to say "He is hard up" to me, I should inquire concerning his plight.

(P_6) If someone were to say "We had a very hard winter" to me, I should be sympathetic to them.

Such rules determine the *practical purposes* sentences 7, 8, and 9 had in James's idiolect.

    Nineteenth-century logicians, in the spirit of Cartesianism, made much of the clarity and distinctness of ideas. When Peirce subjected their views to scrutiny, he found that clarity came down to familiarity as exhibited in fluent usage: "Taking clearness in the sense of familiarity, no idea could be clearer than this. Every child uses it with perfect confidence, never dreaming that he does not understand it."[10] Clarity is knowledge of practical purposes. Thus it is a matter of having internalized pragmatic rules. James is *clear* about the ideas sentences 7,

8, and 9 formulate, but sentences 10, 11, and 12 would be *obscure* to him. If Peirce is to be believed, Cartesian logicians saw their task as that of making clear ideas *distinct*, that is, of eliminating whatever confusions remain concerning their meaning by precisely defining them in abstract terms. They regarded ideas that have not been precisely defined as confused. According to them, a person only understands those ideas that are clear and distinct for him. Peirce disagrees. Like the Cartesians, he does not think that a person understands an idea simply by knowing its practical purposes. Clarity alone can not guarantee understanding. What he disagrees with them about is that abstract definitions are the way to achieve understanding, or *rational cognition*. Peirce had simply seen too many dilettantes who were full of abstract definitions and utterly void of understanding. In his view, rational cognition is inseparably connected to *rational purpose*—just as having a rational cognition of an idea is a matter of knowing its definition in abstract terms for the Cartesian logician, it is a matter of knowing its rational purposes—knowing the criteria governing its uses—for the experimentalist logician. Now James, as well as Peirce and the Cartesians, wanted his ideas to be rational cognitions. But unlike either Peirce or the Cartesians, he seemed to think that for this to be the case, it was simply a matter of being clear about these ideas, of knowing their practical purposes, of having pragmatic rules for them.

And he seems to think of acquiring pragmatic rules as a much more self-conscious process than does Peirce. For instance, when James writes, "Thought in movement has . . . for its only possible motive the attainment of thought at rest. But when our thought about an object has found its rest in belief, then our action on the subject can firmly and safely begin,"[11] he seems to be thinking of thought as a much more intellectual process than it need be according to Peirce's definition. According to James, after long and careful inquiry, our thought finally comes to rest in belief; then we have clarity; then we have pragmatic rules; then our actions "can firmly and safely begin." But for Peirce this has it all backwards. We have more or less unconsciously known the practical purposes of hardness, goodness, reality, etc., since childhood. Such know-how is not a product of self-conscious inquiry; it is a precondition of it.

James says, in terms borrowed from Peirce:

> To attain perfect clearness in our thoughts of an object, then, we need only consider what effects of a conceivably practical kind the object may involve—what sensations we are to expect from it, and what reactions we must prepare. Our conception of these effects, then, is for us the whole

of our conception of the object, so far as that conception has positive significance at all.

    This is the principle of Peirce, the principle of pragmatism.[12]

    But when James says this, we should not be too quick to assume that he and Peirce mean the same thing. We must remember that the terms that Peirce chose to refer to the rational, as opposed to the practical, purposes of an idea were such as to lead an unwary reader to think that he was talking about practical purposes after all. He used these terms: sensible results; what is tangible and conceivably practical; what could make a possible difference in practice; effects that might conceivably have practical bearings; and practical consequences. In any case, his use of such terms seems to have misled James into thinking that there is an inseparable connection between rational cognition and practical purpose.

    James speaks of attaining perfect clearness in our thoughts of an object, but he does not mean by an object anything like what Peirce means. As his examples show, the objects he is thinking of are (declarative) sentences, especially sentences that formulate philosophical propositions: "Material substance exists," "Spiritual substance exists," "God exists," "There is design in nature," "There is free will," and so on. The principle, which James attributes to Peirce, is this: To attain perfect clearness in our thought about a sentence, we need only consider the possible phenomenal worlds in which it is true and what life in such worlds would be like. Our conception of these worlds and these lives is, for us, the whole of our conception of the sentence, so far as that conception has positive significance at all. Clearly, Peirce had no such principle in mind. James has simply changed the subject. Peirce gave us a method of determining what meaning an abstract term has for us. Henceforth, we'll refer to it alone as *Peirce's Principle of Meaning*:

    (PPM)   If one can define accurately all the criteria governing uses to which a predicate can be put, one will have therein a complete definition of the meaning of what it predicates.

    What James refers to as "Peirce's principle" has an altogether different purpose. It formulates a method of determining what credibility a philosophical proposition has for us. To avoid confusion, then, let us relabel it. We'll call it *James's Principle of Credibility*:

(JPC)   If one can define accurately all the possible worlds and possible lives in which a sentence is true, one will have therein a complete account of the credibility of what the sentence says.

When James speaks of *the pragmatic method,* he is referring to applications of this principle in philosophy: It is "primarily a method of settling metaphysical disputes that otherwise might be interminable."[13] It can settle these disputes because "the effective meaning of any philosophic proposition can always be brought down to some particular consequence, in our future practical experience."[14] Futurity comes in because James's conception of possibility is Diodorean; that is, what is *possible* is what either is or will be actual, and what is *possible for* a particular person is what either is or will be actual in that person's lifetime. Hence, according to James, "the whole function of philosophy ought to be to find out what definite difference it will make to you and me, at definite instants of our life, if this world-formula or that world-formula be the one which is true."[15]

The source of *the pragmatic method* in philosophy for James is not Peirce but the British empiricists:

I am happy to say that it is the English-speaking philosophers who first introduced the custom of interpreting the meaning of conceptions by asking what difference they make for life. Mr. Peirce has only expressed in the form of an explicit maxim what their sense for reality led them all instinctively to do. The great English way of investigating a conception is to ask yourself right off, "What is it *known as*? In what facts does it result? What is its *cash-value*, in terms of particular experience? and what special difference would come into the world according as it were true or false?"[16]

James singles out for particular mention Locke's analysis of the concept of personal identity, Berkeley's of "material substance," and Hume's of "causation."[17] "Stewart and Brown, James Mill, John Mill, and Bain have followed more or less consistently the same method; and Shadworth Hodgson has used it almost as explicitly as Mr. Peirce."[18] Remember, "James is thinking about the pragmatic method—the application of JPC— as opposed to what we might call "the experimental method," or the application of PPM. So it might not be surprising that Shadworth Hodgson had used it almost as explicitly as Peirce had—for it's not clear that Peirce ever used it at all, or at all explicitly.

But still, Shadworth Hodgson? When Hodgson received a copy of
Pragmatism—which is subtitled "A New Name for Some Old Ways of
Thinking"—he responded:

London, June 18, 1907

My dear James,—

Many thanks for so kindly sending me your book on *Pragmatism,*
through the London publishers. I shall read it with the greatest plea-
sure and the greatest attention; though I must confess that I am
strongly pre-possessed against what I know are its tenets, and can
hardly imagine it possible that I should be convinced by it. You describe the name "Pragmatism" as a new name for some old ways of
thinking;—I go no farther than your title-page for this. Of course,—*old*
and *ever-recurring.* The names "Pragmatism" and "Humanism" alike
announce its partial character, and therefore its total unfitness to be a
philosophy. How can you dream of elevating the needs, the desires, the
purposes, of Man into a "measure" of the Universe? You have surely
first to ask, what experience *compels him to think of* Man, and the
Universe, and the relation between them, as *really being,* before you
can even ask the question of how much those needs, desires, or purposes, reveal of the nature of the Universe.

But enough of this *old* criticism of an *old* way of thinking. Let me
congratulate you on your election as a corresponding member of the
British Academy. I am greatly rejoiced thereat, as a humble member of
that body. I am, as ever, sincerely yours,

Shadworth H. Hodgson[19]

In light of this, James's remark does seem quite a slap at Peirce. After
all, there is a sense in which the pragmatic method, as well as the
experimental method, can be said to have been derived from Peirce.
"Peirce made James acutely conscious of an idea which he had already
imbibed, and continued to imbibe from many sources," Ralph Barton
Perry notes, and "this idea was to the effect that the meaning of a
concept lay in its putting a particular face on a situation and thereby
provoking a particular action."[20] When the idea is grasped at this level
of generality, then both the experimental and the pragmatic method can
be seen to be applications of Peirce's idea. When the experimentalist
considers the application of a concept in a situation, the face he sees
being put on the situation is that of an *experiment:* For him, the meaning
of the concept lies in its predicting that if a certain experiment—one
in which this application of the concept is put to the test—were to be
performed, there would be a certain experimental result. On the other
hand, when the pragmatist (as James employs the term) considers the

application of a concept, the meaning of the concept lies in its implying that if a certain possible world—one in which this application of the concept *is true*—were to be actualized, there would be certain practical consequences. (The situation suggests a trip into the future [in the spirit of *The Time Machine*, which James's friend H. G. Wells had published in 1894].) So the pragmatist and the experimentalist differ as to what face they see the situation being given, but they are both applying the same idea—Peirce's idea that the meaning of a concept lies in its putting a particular face on a situation, and thereby provoking a particular response. So James's belief does seem a bit nearer to Charles Peirce than to Shadworth Hodgson.

In *Pragmatism*, James also reacted to *Peirce's theory of truth*—

(PTT)   Truth is that to which all scientific investigators are destined to ultimately agree

—as well as to his theory of meaning. (PTT) defines what James calls *absolute truth*:

> The "absolutely" true, meaning what no further experience will ever alter, is that ideal vanishing-point towards which we imagine that all our temporary truths will some day converge. It runs on all fours with the perfectly wise man, and with the absolutely complete experience; and, if these ideals are ever realized, they will all be realized together. Meanwhile we have to live today by what truth we can get today, and be ready tomorrow to call it falsehood.[21]

It is interesting that James quotes Kierkegaard in this connection, to the effect that even though we "understand backward," we must "live forward."[22] One wonders whether he was aware of the following passage, which Kierkegaard italicized in his *Concluding Unscientific Postscript*:

> When the question of truth is raised in an objective manner, reflection is directed objectively to the truth, as an object to which the knower is related. Reflection is not focussed upon the relationship, however, but upon the question of whether it is the truth to which the knower is related. If only the object to which he is related is the truth, the subject is accounted to be in the truth. When the question of the truth is raised subjectively, reflection is directed subjectively to the nature of the individual's rela-tionship; if only the mode of this relationship is in the truth, the individual is in the truth even if he should happen to be thus related to what is not true.[23]

In any case, what James does in *Pragmatism* is raise the question of truth, as Kierkegaard would say, *subjectively*, and as James would say, *pragmatically*. It may well turn out to be the case that no matter what idea we consider, it is true if and only if all scientific investigators are destined to agree to it. But how does that help us today? Let us not forget, as James reminds Peirce, "we have to live today by what truth we can get today, and be ready tomorrow to call it falsehood."

Peirce might prefer to say that we have to live today by what truth science got yesterday. So be it. Studies of the logic of science, "of the conditions under which our sciences have evolved,"[24] have shown that

> most, perhaps all, of our laws are only approximations. The laws themselves, moreover, have grown so numerous that there is no counting them; and so many rival formulations are proposed in all the branches of science that investigators have become accustomed to the notion that no theory is absolutely a transcript of reality, but that any one of them may from some point of view be useful. Their great use is to summarize old facts and to lead to new ones. They are only a man-made language, a conceptual shorthand, as someone calls them, in which we write our reports of nature; and languages, as is well-known, tolerate much choice of expression and many dialects.[25]

In support of this view of the logic of science, James mentions such early scientific instrumentalists as the Austrian physicist Ernst Mach, the French mathematician Henri Poincaré, and the French physicist Pierre Duhem, among others. It is they, according to James, who set the stage for F.C.S. Schiller's humanism ("*Pragmatic method* asserts that what a concept *means* is its consequences. Humanism says that when these are satisfactory, the concept is *true*,"[26] wrote James in 1905–1906) and John Dewey's philosophical instrumentalism, which was then taking shape in Chicago:

> Riding now on the front of this wave of scientific logic Messrs. Schiller and Dewey appear with their pragmatistic account of what truth everywhere signifies. Everywhere, these teachers say, "truth" in our ideas and beliefs means the same thing that it means in science. It means, they say, nothing but this, *that ideas (which themselves are but parts of our experience) become true just in so far as they help us to get into satisfactory relations with other parts of our experience*, to summarize them and get about among them by conceptual short-cuts instead of following the interminable succession of particular phenomena. Any idea upon which we can ride, so to speak; any idea that will carry us prosperously from any one part of our experience to any other part, linking things satisfactorily, working securely, simplifying, saving labor; is true for just so much, true in so far forth, true *instrumentally*.

This is the "instrumental" view of truth taught so successfully at Chicago, the view that truth in our ideas means their power to "work", promulgated so brilliantly at Oxford.[27]

What we have here is a definition of a technical term, the term 'instrumental truth':

(DIT) An idea *is true instrumentally* just insofar as it helps us to get into satisfactory relations with other parts of our experience.

We note that instrumental truth is a matter of degree:

One idea *is truer (instrumentally) than* another if and only if it helps us more than the other idea to get into satisfactory relations with other parts of our experience.

And instrumental truth is a social or communitarian idea: It helps *us*, not simply you or me.

In *Pragmatism*, James uses this concept of instrumental truth as a basis for "a genetic theory of what is meant by truth." According to this theory, the truth of an idea "is not a stagnant property inherent in it. Truth *happens* to an idea. It *becomes* true, is *made* true by events."[28] As we see from the above quoted passage, *becoming true* is, for James, simply a matter of *being true instrumentally*:

(DBT) An idea *is becoming true* if and only if it is true instrumentally.

James sometimes speaks of ideas that are in the process of becoming true as temporary truths ("The 'absolutely' true, meaning what no further experience will ever alter, is that ideal vanishing-point towards which we imagine that all our temporary truths will some day converge"[29]); or as only relatively true; or as only true within certain borders of experience ("Ptolemaic astronomy, euclidean space, aristotelian logic, scholastic metaphysics were expedient for centuries, but human experience has boiled over those limits, and we now call these things only relatively true, or true within those borders of experience. 'Absolutely' they are false"[30]); or as half-truths ("Like the half-truths, the absolute truth will have to be *made*, made as a relation incidental to the growth of a mass of verification-experience, to which the half-true ideas are all along contributing their quota."[31]); or as probable truths ("Her only test of probable truth is what works best in the way of leading us, what fits every part of life best and combines with the collectivity of experience's demands, nothing being omitted."[32]). With all these synonyms for ideas in the truth-process (ideas in the "process of truth's growth,"[33] ideas in the process of "becoming true"[34]), one would not think that these ideas would get confused with *true ideas*. Unfortunately, that is not the case: James sometimes speaks of ideas in the truth-process as simply true! ("In other words, the greatest enemy of any one of our truths may be the rest of our truths."[35]) So one must be careful.

Older ideas in the truth-process—ideas like water's being H_2O, which we have "put on the shelf" (in Wittgenstein's phrase), ideas whose validity we have long accepted and that are never the subjects of inquiry— exert an "absolutely controlling"[36] influence on the process of truth's growth:

> The individual has a stock of old opinions already, but he meets a new experience that puts them to a strain. Somebody contradicts them; or in a reflective moment he discovers that they contradict each other; or he hears of facts with which they are incompatible; or desires arise in him which they cease to satisfy. The result is an inward trouble to which his mind till then had been a stranger, and from which he seeks to escape by modifying his previous mass of opinions. He saves as much of it as he can, for in this matter of belief we are all extreme conservatives. So he tries to change first this opinion, and then that (for they resist change very variously), until at last some new idea comes up which he can graft upon the ancient stock with a minimum of disturbance of the latter, some idea that mediates between the stock and the new experience and runs them into one another most felicitously and expediently.
>
> This new idea is then adopted as the true one. It preserves the older stock of truths with a minimum of modification, stretching them just enough to make them admit the novelty, but conceiving that in ways as familiar as the case leaves possible. An *outrée* explanation, violating all our preconceptions, would never pass for a true account of a novelty. We should scratch round industriously till we found something less eccentric. The most violent revolutions in an individual's beliefs leave most of his old order standing. Time and space, cause and effect, nature and history, and one's own biography remain untouched. New truth is always a go-between, a smoother-over of transitions. It marries old opinion to new fact so as ever to show a minimum of jolt, a maximum of continuity. We hold a theory true just in proportion to its success in solving this "problem of maxima and minima." But success in solving this problem is eminently a matter of approximation. We say this theory solves it on the whole more satisfactorily than that theory; but that means more satisfactorily to ourselves, and individuals will emphasize their points of satisfaction differently. To a certain degree, therefore, everything here is plastic.[37]

People's beliefs at any particular time, James tells us, "are so much experience *funded*."[38] Such funded experience plays a decisive role in the truth-process. As James writes, "truth is made largely out of previous truths."[39] To be in this process is to be pent in "between the whole body of funded truths squeezed from the past and the coercions of the world of sense about him."[40] And the idea is to save as much of the old as possible while accommodating the new.

In the following passage, James frequently speaks of ideas in the process of becoming true as if they simply *were* true. So let the reader beware:

> A new opinion counts as "true" just in proportion as it gratifies the individual's desire to assimilate the novel in his experience to his beliefs in stock. It must both lean on old truth and grasp new fact; and its success (as I said a moment ago) in doing this, is a matter for the individual's appreciation. When old truth grows, then, by new truth's addition, it is for subjective reasons. We are in the process and obey the reasons. That new idea is truest which performs most felicitously its function of satisfying our double urgency. It makes itself true, gets itself classed as true, by the way it works; grafting itself then upon the ancient body of truth, which thus grows much as a tree grows by the activity of a new layer of cambium.
>
> Now Dewey and Schiller proceed to generalize this observation and to apply it to the most ancient parts of truth. They also once were plastic. They also were called true for human reasons. They also mediated between still earlier truths and what in those days were novel observations. Purely objective truth, truth in whose establishment the function of giving human satisfaction in marrying previous parts of experience with newer parts played no role whatever, is nowhere to be found. The reasons why we call things true is the reason why they *are* true, for "to be true" *means* only to perform this marriage-function.
>
> The trail of the human serpent is thus over everything. Truth independent; truth that we *find* merely; truth no longer malleable to human need; truth incorrigible, in a word; such truth exists indeed superabundantly—or is supposed to exist by rationalistically minded thinkers; but then it means only the dead heart of the living tree, and its being there means only that truth also has its paleontology, and its "prescription," and may grow stiff with years of veteran service and petrified in men's regard by sheer antiquity.[41]

It is only in the instrumental sense that one idea is "truer than" another. So too, that idea is "truest" (instrumentally) "which performs most felicitously its function of satisfying our double urgency." Of such an idea, James says that it "makes itself true, gets itself classed as true, by the way it works." Here we are inclined to agree that in actual fact this is what happens. Some hypotheses so out-perform all their competitors that they cease to have competition, are "put on the shelf," or, as James says, "into cold-storage in the encyclopedia."[42] But we must beware. "The trail of the human serpent is . . . over everything" and what performs its function most felicitously today may not do so tomorrow. Yet it does do so today; so we have no choice but to live by it, but as James is ever ready to remind us, we must "be ready tomorrow to call it falsehood." James, like Peirce, is a fallibilist.

James says that those ideas that continue to be truest instrumentally get themselves classed as true; they make themselves true by the way they work. He speaks of this as the process of *verification*: According to James, ideas verify themselves by their ability to run novel experiences into funded experience "most felicitously and expediently" (with "a minimum of modification," "a minimum of jolt," "a minimum distur-bance," and "a maximum of continuity"). But we must be careful—the word 'verification' is not unambiguous. To verify something can mean any of the following things:

1. To prove the truth of that thing; to confirm it.
2. To ascertain the truth, authenticity, or correctness of it.
3. To act as ultimate proof or evidence of it; to serve to confirm it.
4. To substantiate it by oath.

The mechanic verified that the battery was dead (sense 1). The game warden verified our hunting licenses (sense 2). Spud Webb's performance last season verified that small men can play in the N.B.A. (sense 3). The next witness verified the allegation that had just been made (sense 4). It is important to distinguish these senses because critics of Jamesian pragmatism have often misinterpreted James on the issue of verification. For example, no less an expert than Ralph Barton Perry responded to James's argument by saying, "Verification means to me not making the idea true, it is making me know it to be true." Clearly Perry is thinking of verification in sense 1 or sense 2, not in senses 3 or 4. For example, in sense 4, there is no question of the verifier being made to know the truth. He already knows it. That is why he has been called on to make the verification. And, of course, there's no question of the verifier in this sense making the allegation (or whatever) true. It is true already. He knows it. So he can not now be making it true. And what about sense 3? In this sense, the subject *might both* be making the idea true *and* coming to know that it is true. Spud Webb's performance last season made the idea that small men can play in the N.B.A. true, and it may have also made Spud himself know that it is true. Notice further, that it is only in sense 3 that something's performance—its ability to do a job—can verify itself, as James says that ideas, by their performance in running novel experiences into funded experience most felicitously and expediently, *verify themselves*. So clearly, when he speaks in this way,

James means verification in sense 3 and Perry (and a legion of others) have taken him to mean it in sense 1 or 2.

To be sure, there are places in *Pragmatism* where James does speak of verification in sense 1; but this is usually to play down its role. Speaking of our calling something a clock even though we have never verified in sense 1, James says: "The verification of the assumption here means its leading to no frustration or contradiction. Verifi*ability* of wheels and weights and pendulum is as good as verification. . . . Truth lives, in fact, for the most part on the credit system."[43] But when James says such things as "Truth for us is simply a collective name for verification-processes, just as health, wealth, strength, etc., are names for other processes connected with life, and also pursued because it pays to pursue them. Truth is *made*, just as health, wealth, and strength are made, in the course of experience,"[44] he is speaking of verification in sense 3.

In that sense, as we have seen, ideas are said to verify themselves by mediating between funded and new experiences most felicitously and expediently. And it is verification in this sense that anchors truth in Jamesian pragmatism: "The truth of an idea is not a stagnant property inherent in it. Truth *happens* to an idea. It *becomes* true, is *made* true by events. Its verity *is* in fact an event, a process: the process namely of its verifying itself, its veri-*fication*."[45] And since this is a matter of performing a certain welcoming function expediently, the thoughts from which these ideas arise may also be said to be true if expedient—with certain qualifications, of course:

> 'The true,' to put it very briefly, is only the expedient in the way of our thinking, just as 'the right' is only the expedient in the way of our behaving. Expedient in almost any fashion; and expedient in the long run and on the whole of course; for what meets expediently all the experience in sight won't necessarily meet all farther experiences equally satisfactorily. Experience, as we know, has ways of *boiling over*, and making us correct our present formulas.[46]

The principle is as follows:

1. What is true in our way of thinking is what is expedient on the whole and in the long run.

The decision James made to put such emphasis on 'expedience' may have been an error. For the word is ambiguous: It often means "political rather than just," and this sense of the term not infrequently casts a shadow over discussions of pragmatism. But James meant nothing of the sort. His sense of 'expedience' has to do with suitability or appropriateness. The dictionary defines this sense of 'expedient' as "advantageous, suitable;" James might say "advantageous because suitable."

Since our way of thinking "can never be made to direct itself towards anything but the production of belief," one might wish to point out to James that

2. What is expedient on the whole and in the long run in our way of thinking is the production of beliefs that are true.

And he would no doubt accept the suggestion and try to find the pragmatic meaning in it. What is one saying of a belief in saying that it is true? James's response is that

truth is *one species of good*, and not, as is usually supposed, a category distinct from good, and coordinate with it. *The true is the name of whatever proves itself to be good in the way of belief, and good, too, for definite, assignable reasons.* Surely you must admit this, that if there were *no* good for life in true ideas, or if the knowledge of them were positively disadvantageous and false ideas the only useful ones, then the current notion that truth is divine and precious, and its pursuit a duty, could never have grown up or become a dogma. In a world like that, our duty would be to *shun* truth, rather. But in this world, just as certain foods are not only agreeable to our taste, but good for teeth, our stomach, and our tissues; so certain ideas are not only agreeable as supporting other ideas that we are fond of, but they are helpful in life's practical struggles. If there be any life that it is really better we should lead, and if there be any idea which, if believed in, would help us to lead that life, then it would be really *better for us* to believe in that idea, *unless, indeed, belief in it incidentally clashed with other greater vital benefits.*[47]

The principle here is:

3. The beliefs that prove themselves to be good, and good for definite, assignable reasons, are the true ones.

James continues:

'What would be better for us to believe'! This sounds very like a definition of truth. It comes very near to saying 'what we *ought* to believe': and in *that* definition none of you would find any oddity. Ought we ever not to believe what it *is better for us* to believe? And can we then keep the notion of what is better for us, and what is true for us, permanently apart?

Pragmatism says no, and I fully agree with her.[48]

James's theory of truth is a consequence of principles 1, 2, and 3:

(JTT) What is true in our way of thinking is the production of beliefs that prove themselves to be good, and good for definite, assignable reasons.

This, one might say, is the principle of James, a principle of pragmatism.

CHAPTER SIX

Deweyan Pragmatism

John Dewey was born in 1859, two decades after Charles Peirce. What is more significant is that he died in 1952, *over four decades* after William James. And he was intellectually and politically active until the very end of his life. Unlike either James (who died in 1910) or Peirce (who died in 1914), John Dewey was a man of the twentieth century. Here are a few of the people, places, and events that neither James nor Peirce knew of, but that formed part of the cultural background for Dewey's thoughts: World War I, Lawrence of Arabia, Woodrow Wilson, Pancho Villa, Teddy Roosevelt, behaviorism, James Joyce, Robert Frost, Tarzan, the general theory of relativity, George Gershwin, the Panama Canal, the Russian Revolution, Trotsky, Jack Dempsey, Margaret Sanger, Lenin, the USSR, prohibition, air mail, Knute Rockne, RCA, Babe Ruth, rocketry, Count Rutherford, Arthur Eddington, Jim Thorpe, the American Legion, Bill Tilden, Man o'War, the BBC, the League of Nations, Charlie Chaplin, Joseph Conrad, Irving Berlin, *Birth of a Nation*, D. H. Lawrence, jazz, chromosomes, isotypes, insulin, Norman Thomas, Pavlov, the Scopes trial, dadaism, Matisse, Frank Lloyd Wright, T. S. Eliot, the Empire State Building, the Hindenberg, Sacco and Vanzetti, the Unknown Soldier, the KKK, Emily Post, the Chicago World's Fair, Picasso, Al Jolson, Modigliani, Ludwig Wittgenstein, *Time*, the Four Horsemen of Notre Dame, the Winter Olympics, Bauhaus, Paul Klee, Monet, Agatha Christie, Franz Kafka, Carl Jung, Adolf Hitler, Winston Churchill, Black Friday, the Great Depression, Franklin Roosevelt, the New Deal, German concentration camps, Rudolf Carnap, Marc Chagall, E. E. Cummings, Noel Coward, *The New Yorker*, Ernest Hemingway, Greta Garbo, the Book-of-the-Month Club, William Faulkner, Duke Ellington, Rogers and Hart, Dorothy Sayers, Mickey Mouse, Walter Lippmann, the Vienna Circle, Salvador Dali, the Museum of Modern Art, Aaron Copland, the Manhattan Project, Cole Porter, *The Maltese Falcon*, General MacArthur, Pearl Harbor, Iwo Jima, the Battle of the Bulge, Hiroshima, D-Day, Eisenhower, plastic, splitting the atom, Yalta, helicopters, FM radio, Alfred Hitchcock, the

Jehovah's Witnesses, Clark Gable, Shirley Temple, King Kong, swing, A. J. Ayer, Rogers and Hammerstein, Sartre, Donald Duck, Orson Welles, Benny Goodman, *Gone With the Wind, The Wizard of Oz,* the Marx Brothers, the All-American Football Team, the Harlem Globetrotters, Charles Lindbergh, Al Capone, the *Queen Mary,* the St. Valentine's Day Massacre, Joe Louis, the FBI, the CIA, *Life,* the Golden Gate Bridge, the *Queen Elizabeth,* Pan American Airways, fighter planes, Jack Benny, radar, nylon, Mae West, television, Bambi, Jackson Pollock, Hank Williams, cyclotrons, penicillin, computers, jet planes, the Nuremberg trials, George Orwell, Robert Penn Warren, Dr. Spock, Lawrence Durrell, Martin Buber, Henry Moore, Whirlaway, zoot suits, bebop, flying saucers, Citation, Gilbert Ryle, Bogart, Brando, Leadbelly, transistors, guided missiles, antihistamines, oral contraceptives, Truman Capote, Grace Kelly, the Iron Curtain, apartheid, the hydrogen bomb, Eddie Arcaro, Joe DiMaggio, color TV, Jackie Robinson, Joe McCarthy, and Rocky Marciano.

John Dewey was a twentieth-century philosopher. He was a college professor, who taught for ten years at the University of Michigan (1884–1894), ten years at the University of Chicago (1894–1904), and twenty-six years at Columbia University (1904–1930). Between 1884 and 1898, he published pioneering work in the new field of psychology, for which he was elected president of the American Psychological Association in 1899–1900. He was elected president of the American Philosophical Association six years later in 1905–1906; and he became the first president of the American Association of University Professors (an organization he had helped to found) in 1915. His best philosophical work, published during the following quarter century, included the following books: *Democracy and Education* (1916); *Reconstruction in Philosophy* (1920); *Human Nature and Conduct* (1922); *Experience and Nature* (1925); *The Quest for Certainty* (1929); *Art as Experience* (1934); and *Logic: The Theory of Inquiry* (1938).

In 1919, Dewey lectured in Japan, and then, for two years, in China. In 1924, he made an inspection tour of the schools in Turkey, in 1926, those in Mexico, and in 1928, those in the Soviet Union. And he did not retire from Columbia University until 1930!

As those educational surveys in Turkey, Mexico, and the Soviet Union would indicate, John Dewey was an internationally known educational theorist, as well as a philosopher and psychologist. At the University of Chicago, he was chairman of the Department of Philosophy, Psychology, and Education, and it was then that he founded and directed the Experimental School of Chicago. As Sidney Hook tells us,

An imposing galaxy of scientists and philosophers from the University of Chicago co-operated in elaborating the curriculum, adapting it to various age levels, and also in teaching. Among them were the geologist, Chamberlin, originator of the planetesimal hypothesis of the earth's origin; Michelson, the physicist; Coulter, in botany; Whitman, in zoology; Jacques Loeb, in physiology; A. Smith, in chemistry; W. I. Thomas, in sociology; and G. H. Mead, J. H. Tufts, and J. R. Angell, in philosophy.[1]

For Dewey, the problems of education were an opportunity to test philosophical and psychological, as well as purely educational, ideas. Sidney Hook says categorically, "The Dewey Laboratory School was the most important experimental venture in the whole history of American education."[2] It was while involved with the Laboratory School that Dewey wrote *The School and Society* (1900) and *The Child and the Curriculum* (1902). When he left Chicago for Columbia University in 1904, Dewey already had a national reputation as an educational theorist. While at Columbia, his reputation became international, mainly through his influence on the Columbia Teachers College, which became a training center for teachers from around the world. It was through graduates of the Teachers College more than through his later books on education— *How We Think* (1910), *Democracy and Education* (1916), and *Experience and Education* (1938)—that Dewey's educational philosophy spread throughout the world. That philosophy sees education as "a continuous reconstruction of experience in which there is a development of immature experience toward experience funded with the skills and habits of intelligence."[3] Dewey saw the school as a possibly ideal society that all citizens would experience at an impressionable age. Thus he saw it as the principal means for social reform in a democratic society. Richard Bernstein says that the school, for Dewey, "is the most important medium for strengthening and developing a genuine democratic community, and the task of democracy is forever the creation of a freer and more humane experience in which all share and participate."[4] Sidney Hook observes that "only to the extent that foreign nations were committed to the democratic way of life, could Dewey's educational theories be put into practice."[5]

John Dewey was educated at the University of Vermont (B.A., 1879) and the Johns Hopkins University (Ph.D., 1884). During his undergraduate years, Dewey had first grasped the importance of the concept of *the organic* from studying the evolutionary writings of "Darwin's bulldog," T. H. Huxley; his graduate education gave expression to that early interest in "the interdependence and interrelated unity of all things" in Hegelian terms—terms, he said, that left "a permanent deposit" in his thinking.[6] Charles Peirce had taught at Johns Hopkins from 1880 to 1884, and Dewey took two courses from him. Nonetheless, Dewey said that it was not until many years later that he became aware of Peirce's vast learning and his importance as a philosopher. What Dewey remembered was Peirce's criticisms of atomistic theories of consciousness. To Dewey, "Peirce seemed to be suggesting a conception of the life of the mind as a series of flights and perches in the stream of consciousness"[7]—a conception that William James was to develop so brilliantly in his *Principles of Psychology*, published in 1890. That book had an enormous influence on Dewey during his Chicago days. In *Studies in Logical Theory* (1903), Dewey and his fellow instrumentalists of the Chicago School "recognized how much they owed to William James for having forged the instruments which they used."[8] In "The Development of American Pragmatism" Dewey points out that

> it is curious to note that the "instruments" to which allusion is made, are not the considerations which were of the greatest service to James. They precede his pragmatism and it is among some of the pages of his *Principles of Psychology* that one must look for them. This important work (1890) really developed two distinct theses.
>
> The one is a re-interpretation of introspective psychology, in which James denies that sensations, images and ideas are discrete and in which he replaces them by a continuous stream which he calls "the stream of consciousness." . . .
>
> The other aspect of his *Principles of Psychology* is of a biological nature. It shows itself in its full force in the criterion which James established for discovering the existence of mind. "The pursuance of future ends and the choice of means for their attainment are thus the mark and criterion of the presence of mentality in a phenomenon. The force of this criterion is plainly shown in . . . the chapter on Conception, where he shows that a general idea is a mode of signifying particular things and not merely an abstraction from particular cases or a super-empirical function,—that it is a teleological instrument. James then develops this idea in the chapter on reasoning where he says that "the only meaning of essences is teleological, and that classification and conception are purely teleological weapons of mind."[9]

When the Chicago instrumentalists set out to develop a logical theory of conception and judgment, they did so from this Jamesian point of view, and this resulted in a theory of intelligence of the following sort:

> The adaptations made by inferior organisms, for example, their effective and coordinated responses to stimuli, become teleological in man and therefore give occasion to thought. Reflection is an indirect response to the environment, and the element of indirection can itself become great and very complicated. But it has its origin in biological adaptive behaviour and the ultimate function of its cognitive aspect is a prospective control of the conditions of the environment. The function of intelligence is

therefore not that of copying the objects of the environment, but rather of taking account of the ways in which more effective and more profitable relations with these objects may be established in the future.[10]

Thus, the instrumentalism that so influenced Jamesian pragmatism turns out to have been an outgrowth and application of James's own teleological theory of mind.

When Dewey came to a full appreciation of the philosophical importance of both Peirce and James, it was for their foresight and courage in virtually single-handedly opposing the depreciation of action—of doing and making—that had been characteristic of the Western philosophical tradition since the time of Plato and Aristotle. Dewey examines this depreciation in an essay of 1929, "Escape from Peril." He speculates on the reasons why the classical Greek philosophers came up with

the idea of a higher realm of fixed reality of which alone true science is possible and of an inferior world of changing things with which experience and practical matters are concerned. They glorified the invariant at the expense of change, it being evident that all practical activity falls within the realm of change. They bequeathed the notion, which has ruled philosophy ever since the time of the Greeks, that the office of knowledge is to uncover the antecedently real, rather than, as is the case with our practical judgments, to gain the kind of understanding which is necessary to deal with problems as they arise.[11]

This was the tide against which Peirce and James had dared to swim.

But, for Dewey, it was not the arguments of Peirce and James but those of Charles Darwin that actually tolled the death knell for the Greek glorification of being over becoming and of knowledge over justified belief. As Dewey points out in "The Influence of Darwinism on Philosophy" (1925), the very combination of the words 'origin' and 'species' embodied an intellectual revolt and introduced a new intellectual temper. For the word 'species' is derived from the scholastic translation of the Greek word that, with Plato and Aristotle, came to denote those fixed realities that were genuine objects of knowledge. Once species themselves had been brought into the world of change, once they came into and went out of existence, philosophers could no longer feel justified in assuming the superiority of the fixed and final, and change and origin could no longer be justifiably treated as signs of defect and unreality. For Dewey, the influence of Darwinism on philosophy "resided in its having conquered the phenomena of life for the principle of transition, and thereby freed the new logic for application to mind and morals and life."[12] It was Peirce and James who first realized this and who began making the application. Dewey summarizes these developments in "The Development of American Pragmatism."

Dewey, like Peirce, saw himself as an experimentalist. Remember that when Peirce opposed the spirit of Cartesianism to that of experimentalism, he argued that, as to its methods, philosophy ought to imitate rather than criticize the successful sciences; such a philosophical methodology presupposed a quite different concept of experience than that which the philosophical tradition had bequeathed. John Dewey spent much of his philosophical career formulating and refining just such a concept of experience. Although it is the key conception in his philosophy, *experience* may have been his nemesis as well. It had become a deeply entrenched term of art in philosophy, and Dewey came to believe it had been "a piece of historic folly" to think that he could change all that.[13] As you would expect, the philosophical term was ambiguous. The Hegelian tradition took experience to be a single, dynamic, unified whole in which everything is ultimately interrelated. This is Dewey's original (philosophical) concept of experience. It is the "absolutely complete experience" that James says runs on all fours with the absolutely true idea and the perfectly wise man. For "if these ideals are ever realized, they will all be realized together." But the Cartesian tradition (including the British empiricists) took experience to be a sequence of ideas or sensations that are *of*, but not *in*, nature. Dewey would have none of this will-o'-the-wisp experience. The most that can be said about the purely given element in experience that the Cartesian sought to isolate is that it is, as James says, "a blooming, buzzing confusion."[14] Experimentalism demands a much more stable and much richer concept of experience than that—even if not an idealization such as the Hegelians had proposed. Dewey had hoped to redeem such philosophical usage of the word 'experience' by returning this term to its ordinary, idiomatic usage, as when we speak of someone as an experienced carpenter or say that someone has had a lot of experience with Volkswagen transmissions. In this usage, experience is familiarity with a matter of practical concern, based on repeated past acquaintance or performance. To have experience, in this sense, one has to have had experiences—events or sequences of events that one has participated in or at least lived through. It is this ordinary idea of experience that underlay Greek philosophy, too: Aristotle meant by 'experience' *the capacity to do something*, a capacity acquired by doing that thing repeatedly, guided by rule-of-thumb precepts (Kant's pragmatic rules) rather than by theoretical understanding. Dewey's claim is that not only the craftsman's skill and the practical man's wisdom, but the scientist's knowledge are based on experience in this quite ordinary sense of the term. As Bernstein says:

Dewey thought of himself as part of a general movement that was developing a new empiricism based on a new concept of experience, one that combined the strong, naturalistic bias of the Greek philosophers with a sensitive appreciation for experimental method as practiced by the sciences. He was sympathetic with what he took to be the Greek view of experience, which considers it as consisting of a fund of social knowledge and skills and as being the means by which man comes into direct contact with a qualitatively rich and variegated nature. But Dewey was just as forceful in pointing out that this view of experience had to be reconstructed in light of the experimental method of the sciences.[15]

Dewey came to view experience as one of three types of *natural transitions* (naturally occurring actions in which the components and elements involved both condition and are conditioned by the entire coordination). Among such organic coordinations, some are simply *physiochemical transactions*, as when an organ secretes an enzyme that breaks the biochemical products of stress down into excretable form; some are *psychophysical transactions*, as when an animal feels a pain in its belly; and some are *experiential transactions*, as when a human being takes an antacid to relieve stomach pain. The distinguishing characteristics of human experiences (experiential transactions) are found by studying the modes of societal life—and, particularly, the modes of linguistic communication—that human beings have developed. We noted earlier that to have experience in the Greek sense, to have a fund of social knowledge and skills by means of which one comes into contact with a rich and variegated natural world, one has to have had experiences. Dewey explains what it means to have *an* experience—as opposed to merely undergoing certain things or to disposing of them in a mechanical way—in the third chapter of *Art as Experience*, "Having an Experience." This is an exquisite piece of philosophy, as good as anything Dewey ever produced. It focuses on the sort of experience that is both artistic (which refers primarily to the production of art) and aesthetic (which refers primarily to the perception and enjoyment of art).[16] Dewey calls it *esthetic experience*, and so will we, putting a variation in spelling to good use. Dewey's main point is that "the esthetic is no intruder in experience from without, whether by way of idle luxury or transcendent ideality, but that it is the clarified and intensified development of traits that belong to every normally complete experience."[17] We know that conversation is an art—for Dewey, all thought and inquiry, when well-conducted, is an art. Indeed, life itself, when well-lived, has an artistic quality. Dewey's point is that the fine arts themselves—literature, painting, sculpture, music, dance, and so on—differ only in degree, not in kind, from the other aspects of a well-lived life.

The qualification "well-lived" is necessary because there are many lives in which experience does not often mature into integral experiences. In such lives, things "are experienced but not in such a way that they are composed into *an* experience."[18] Such experience fails to reach "the end for the sake of which it was initiated."[19] In contrast, "we have *an* experience when the material experienced runs its course to fulfillment. Then and then only is it integrated within and demarcated in the general stream of experience from other experiences."[20] Dewey illustrates the point with an example of an interview situation:

Two men meet; one is the applicant for a position, while the other has the disposition of the matter in his hands. The interview may be mechanical, consisting of set questions, the replies to which perfunctorily settle the matter. There is no experience in which the two men meet, nothing that is not a repetition, by way of acceptance or dismissal, of something which has happened a score of times. The situation is disposed of as if it were an exercise in bookkeeping. But an interplay may take place in which a new experience develops. Where should we look for an account of such an experience? Not to ledger-entries nor yet to a treatise on economics or sociology or personnel-psychology, but to drama or fiction. Its nature and import can be expressed only by art, because there is a unity of experience that can be expressed only as an experience. The *experience* is of material fraught with suspense and moving toward its own consummation through a connected series of varied incidents. The primary emotions on the part of the applicant may be at the beginning hope or despair, and elation or disappointment at the close. These emotions qualify the experience as a unity. But as the interview proceeds, secondary emotions are evolved as variations of the primary underlying one. It is even possible for each attitude and gesture, each sentence, almost every word, to produce more than a fluctuation in the intensity of the basic emotion; to produce, that is, a change of shade and tint in its quality. The employer sees by means of his own emotional reactions the character of the one applying. He projects him imaginatively into the work to be done and judges his fitness by the way in which the elements of the scene assemble and either clash or fit together. The presence and behavior of the applicant either harmonize with his own attitudes and desires or they conflict and jar. Such factors as these, inherently esthetic in quality, are the forces that carry the varied elements of the interview to a decisive issue. They enter into the settlement of every situation, whatever its dominant nature, in which there are uncertainty and suspense.[21]

Vital, mature experiences are not only consummatory; they are integral: Each "has a unity that gives it its name, *that* meal, that storm, that rupture of friendship. The existence of this unity is constituted by a single *quality* that pervades the entire experience in spite of the variation of its constituent parts."[22] It was a frightening experience, a horrendous experience, a religious experience, and so on. The unifying quality of an experience is an emotional quality, an esthetic quality. To have such a quality, an experience must be such that each of its constituent actions is linked in anticipation to its outcome for sense. When an experience has such an esthetic quality what is done and what is undergone in it are "reciprocally, cumulatively, and continuously instrumental to each other."[23] Esthetic experience results from "the clarified and intensified development of traits that belong to every normally complete experience."[24]

There are many modes of experiencing, some cognitive, some not. Peirce was insightful in singling out the mode of experiencing called *inquiry* for special attention in philosophy. "Many definitions of mind and thinking have been given," Dewey says in "The Supremacy of Method" (1929), and he adds, "I know of but one that goes to the heart of the matter:—response to the doubtful as such,"[25] which, of course, is Peirce's definition of thought. In "The Postulate of Immediate Empiricism" (1905) Dewey says that the process of inquiry is that specific way of having experience in which things are "experienced as known things," as compared with "things experienced esthetically, or morally, or economically or technically."[26] Idealism had fallen into the error of identifying experience with cognitive experience. It is to this fallacy that Dewey is responding in the following passage:

> By our postulate, things are what they are experienced to be; and unless knowing is the sole and only genuine mode of experiencing, it is fallacious to say that Reality is just and exclusively what it is or would be to an all-competent all-knower; or even that it *is* relatively and piece-meal, what it is to a finite and partial knower. Or, put more positively, knowing is one mode of experiencing, and the primary philosophic demand (from the standpoint of immediatism) is to find out *what* sort of an experience knowing is—or, concretely how things are experienced when they are experienced *as* known things.[27]

Affirmation of non-cognitive experience is thematic in Dewey's writings.

In "Experience and Philosophic Method," Dewey refers to the idealists' fallacy as an arbitrary "intellectualism" and says that it is "the great vice of philosophy":

> By "intellectualism" as an indictment is meant the theory that all experiencing is a mode of knowing, and that all subject-matter, all nature, is, in principle, to be reduced and transformed till it is defined in terms identical with the characteristics presented by refined objects of science as such. The assumption of "intellectualism" goes contrary to the facts of

what is primarily experienced. For things are objects to be treated, used, acted upon or with, enjoyed and endured, even more than things to be known. They are things *had* before they are things cognized.[28]

What are *primarily experienced,* according to Dewey, are scraped knees, umbrellas, orders from the boss, dancing partners, fajitas, the June rains in San Antonio, and so on. Even more than things to be known, they are things to be *treated* ("Oh, that must really hurt. Come on, I'll put some medicine on it—it will take the fire out of it."), *used* ("I need one small enough to fit in my briefcase. Otherwise, I never have it when I need it."), *acted upon* ("Hi, I want to order a cap and gown for the fall convocation."), *acted with* ("My heavens, this is a waltz! I've been trying to two-step to it."), *enjoyed* ("Shall we order another half pound?"), endured ("Well, at least I remembered to bring my umbrella today."), etc. For things to be known: I even have to stop and think about what it means to say that *I know* a scraped knee ("I know a scraped knee when I see one.") or an umbrella ("I know umbrellas. I'll pick out a good one for you.") or an order ("*This* is not a request. I know an order when I see one.") or a dancing partner ("I know Anna. She'll love to dance to this.") or fajitas ("Look, I know fajitas, these are terrible; they've hardly been marinated.") or San Antonio's June rains ("I know them well; I've lived here for years."). "They are things had before they are things cognized."

Dewey contrasts primary ("direct") experience with secondary ("reflective") experience. The objects of secondary experience are theoretical entities. In "Experience and Philosophic Method," Dewey describes

the relationship between the objects of primary and of secondary or reflective experience. That the subject-matter of primary experience sets the problems and furnishes the first data of the reflection which constructs the secondary objects is evident; it is also obvious that test and verification of the latter is secured only by return to things of crude or macroscopic experience—the sun, earth, plants and animals of common, every-day life. But just what role do the objects attained in reflection play? Where do they come in? They *explain* the primary objects, they enable us to grasp them with *understanding,* instead of just having sense-contact with them. But how?

Well, they define or lay out a path by which return to experienced things is of such a sort that the meaning, the significant content, of what is experienced gains an enriched and expanded force because of the path or method by which it was reached. Directly, in immediate contact it may be just what it was before—hard, colored, odorous, etc. But when the secondary objects, the refined objects, are employed as a method or road for coming at them, these qualities cease to be isolated details; they get

the meaning contained in a whole system of related objects; they are
rendered continuous with the rest of nature and take on the import of
the things they are now seen to be continuous with. The phenomena
observed in the eclipse tested and, as far as they went, confirmed Einstein's
theory of deflection of light by mass. But that is far from being the whole
story. The phenomena themselves got a far-reaching significance they did
not previously have. Perhaps they would not even have been noticed if
the theory had not been employed as a guide or road to observation of
them. But even if they had been noticed, they would have been dismissed
as of no importance, just as we daily drop from attention hundreds of
perceived details for which we have no intellectual use. But approached
by means of theory these lines of slight deflection take on a significance
as large as that of the revolutionary theory that led to their being
experienced.[29]

The charge that Dewey "brought against the non-empirical method of
philosophizing is not that it depends upon theorizing, but that it fails
to use refined, secondary products as a path pointing and leading back
to something in primary experience."[30] As "a first-rate test of the value
of any philosophy which is offered us," Dewey suggests the following
questions:

Does it end in conclusions which, when they are referred back to ordinary
life-experiences and their predicaments, render them more significant, more
luminous to us, and make our dealings with them more fruitful? Or does
it terminate in rendering the things of ordinary experience more opaque
than they were before, and in depriving them of having in "reality" even
the significance they had previously seemed to have? Does it yield the
enrichment and increase of power of ordinary things which the results of
physical science afford when applied in every-day affairs? Or does it
become a mystery that these ordinary things should be what they are;
and are philosophic concepts left to dwell in separation in some technical
realm of their own? It is the fact, I repeat, that so many philosophies
terminate in conclusions that make it necessary to disparage and condemn
primary experience, leading those who hold them to measure the sublimity
of their "realities" as philosophically defined by remoteness from the
concerns of daily life, which leads cultivated common-sense to look askance
at philosophy.[31]

This test might be called *Dewey's Principle of Credibility*.

In contrast to the traditional ("non-empirical") method of philosophizing, the empirical method Dewey advocates exacts two things of
philosophy: "First, that refined methods and products be traced back to
their origin in primary experience in all its heterogeneity and fullness;
so that the needs and problems out of which they arise and which they

have to satisfy be acknowledged. Secondly, that the secondary methods and conclusions be brought back to the things of ordinary experience, in all their coarseness and crudity, for verification."[32] When philosophy lives up to these standards, Dewey tells us, there is a special service that it may render:

> Empirically pursued it will not be a study of philosophy but a study, by means of philosophy, of life-experience. But this experience is already overlaid and saturated with the products of the reflection of past generations and by-gone ages. It is filled with interpretations, classifications, due to sophisticated thought, which have become incorporated into what seems to be fresh, naive empirical material. It would take more wisdom than is possessed by the wisest historic scholar to track all of these absorbed borrowings to their original sources. If we may for the moment call these materials prejudices (even if they are true, as long as their source and authority is unknown), then philosophy is a critique of prejudices. These incorporated results of past reflection, welded into the genuine materials of first-hand experience, may become organs of enrichment if they are detected and reflected upon. If they are not detected, they often obfuscate and distort. Clarification and emancipation follow when they are detected and cast out; and one great object of philosophy is to accomplish this task.
>
> An empirical philosophy is in any case a kind of intellectual disrobing. We cannot permanently divest ourselves of the intellectual habits we take on and wear when we assimilate the culture of our own time and place. But intelligent furthering of culture demands that we take some of them off, that we inspect them critically to see what they are made of and what wearing them does to us. We cannot achieve recovery of primitive naïveté. But there is attainable a cultivated naïveté of eye, ear and thought, one that can be acquired only through the discipline of severe thought.[33]

Dewey's writings, over many decades, exhibit just such a cultivated naïveté of eye, ear, and thought.

In *The Quest for Certainty* Dewey is disrobing our life-experience of some of the effects of those "traditional theories of mind and its organs of knowledge [that] isolate them from continuity with the natural world,"[34] with which it is overlaid and saturated. Such intellectual disrobing often takes place by means of a contrast. For example, in "The Supremacy of Method," such transcendental theories of mind are contrasted with Charles Peirce's empirical theory:

> We do not need to repeat the results of the previous discussion. They are all connected with the theory that inquiry is a set of operations in which problematic situations are disposed of or settled. Theories which have been criticized all rest upon a different supposition; namely, that the

properties of the states and acts of mind involved in knowing are capable of isolated determination—of description apart from overt acts that resolve indeterminate and ambiguous situations. The fundamental advantage of framing our account of the organs and processes of knowing on the pattern of what occurs in experimental inquiry is that nothing is introduced save what is objective and is accessible to examination and report.[35]

Dewey continues:

Our discussion involves a summary as well as some repetition of points previously made. Its significance lies in the liberation which comes when knowing, in all its phases, conditions and organs, is understood after the pattern provided by experimental inquiry, instead of upon the groundwork of ideas framed before such knowing had a systematic career opened to it. For according to the pattern set by the practice of knowing, knowledge is the fruit of the undertakings that transform a problematic situation into a resolved one. Its procedure is public, a part and partner of the Nature in which all interactions exist. But experienced situations come about in two ways and are of two distinct types. Some take place with only a minimum of regulation, with little foresight, preparation and intent. Others occur because, in part, of the prior occurrence of intelligent action. Both kinds are *had*; they are undergone, enjoyed or suffered. The first are not known; they are not understood; they are dispensations of fortune or providence. The second have, as they are experienced, meanings that present the funded outcome of operations that substitute definite continuity for experienced discontinuity and for the fragmentary quality due to isolation. Dream, insanity and fantasy are natural products, as "real" as anything else in the world. The acts of intentional regulation which constitute thinking are also natural developments, and so are the experienced things in which they eventuate. But the latter are resolutions of the problems set by objects experienced without intent and purpose; hence they have a security and fullness of meaning the first lack. Nothing happens, as Aristotle and the scholastics said, without an end—without a terminal effectuation. *Every* experienced object is, in some sense, such a closing and consummatory closing episode: alike the doubtful and secure, the trivial and significant, the true and mistaken, the confused and ordered. Only when the ends are closing termini of *intelligent operations* of thinking are they ends in the honorific sense. We always experience individual objects, but only the individual things which are fruits of intelligent action have in them intrinsic order and fullness of qualities.[36]

Dewey then draws a conclusion concerning the relation of knowledge and action from his refinement of the Peircean theory of mind. "The distinction once made between theory and practice has meaning as a distinction between two kinds of action: blind and intelligent. Intelligence is a quality of some acts, those which are directed; and directed action is an achievement not an original endowment."[37]

This conclusion, Dewey goes on to say, is decisive for the significance of both mechanism and purpose in the natural world:

> The doctrine that knowledge is ideally or in its office a disclosure of antecedent reality resulted, under the impact of the results of natural science, in relegating purpose to the purely subjective, to states of consciousness. An unsolved problem then developed out of the question as to how purposes could be efficacious in the world. Now intelligent action is purposive action; if it is a natural occurrence, coming into being under complex but specifiable conditions of organic and social interaction, then purpose like intelligence is within nature; it is a "category" having objective standing and validity. It has this status in a direct way through the place and operation of human art within the natural scene; for distinctively human conduct can be interpreted and understood only in terms of purpose. Purpose is the dominant category of anything truly denominated history, whether in its enacting or in the writing of it, since action which is *distinctively* human is marked by intent.
>
> Indirectly, purpose is a legitimate and necessary idea in describing Nature itself in the large. For man is continuous with nature. As far as natural events culminate in the intelligent arts of mankind, nature itself has a history, a movement toward consequences.[38]

Finally, this analysis is allowed to shed light on the nature of human freedom:

> No mechanically exact science of an individual is possible, an individual is a history unique in character. But constituents of an individual are known when they are regarded not as qualitative, but as statistical constants derived from a series of operations.
>
> This fact has an obvious bearing on freedom in action. Contingency is a necessary although not, in a mathematical phrase, a sufficient condition of freedom. In a world which was completely tight and exact in all its constituents, there would be no room for freedom. Contingency while it gives room for freedom does not fill that room. Freedom is an actuality when the recognition of relations, the stable element, is combined with the uncertain element, in the knowledge which makes foresight possible and secures intentional preparation for probable consequences. We are free in the degree in which we act knowing what we are about. The identification of freedom with "freedom of will" locates contingency in the wrong place. Contingency of will would mean that uncertainty was uncertainly dealt with; it would be a resort to chance for a decision. The business of "will" is to be resolute; that is, to resolve, under the guidance of thought, the indeterminateness of uncertain *situations*. Choice wavers and is brought

to a head arbitrarily only when circumstances compel action and yet we have no intelligent clew as to how to act.

The doctrine of "free-will" is a desperate attempt to escape from the consequences of the doctrine of fixed and immutable objective Being. With dissipation of that dogma, the need for such a measure of desperation vanishes. Preferential activities characterize every individual as individual or unique. In themselves these are differential in a *de facto* sense. They become true choices under the direction of insight. Knowledge, instead of revealing a world in which preference is an illusion and does not count or make a difference, puts in our possession the instrumentality by means of which preference may be an intelligent or intentional factor in constructing a future by wary and prepared action. Knowledge of special conditions and relations is instrumental to the action which is in turn an instrument of production of situations having qualities of added significance and order. To be capable of such action is to be free.[39]

In "The Construction of Good" Dewey is disrobing human experience of the intellectual habits in which both transcendental and empirical theories of value have clothed it. For example:

The formal statement may be given concrete content by pointing to the difference between the enjoyed and the enjoyable, the desired and the desirable, the satis*fying* and the satis*factory*. To say that something is enjoyed is to make a statement about a fact, something already in existence; it is not to judge the value of that fact. There is no difference between such a proposition and one which says that something is sweet or sour, red or black. It is just correct or incorrect and that is the end of the matter. But to call an object a value is to assert that it satisfies or fulfills certain conditions. Function and status in meeting conditions is a different matter from bare existence. The fact that something is desired only raises the *question* of its desirability; it does not settle it. Only a child in the degree of his immaturity thinks to settle the question of desirability by reiterated proclamation: "I want it, I want it, I want it." What is objected to in the current empirical theory of values is not connection of them with desire and enjoyment but failure to distinguish between enjoyments of radically different sorts.[40]

Of course, Dewey's theory of value is also empirical. His idea is that the development of good taste is at the heart of the matter:

The word "taste" has perhaps got too completely associated with arbitrary liking to express the nature of judgments of value. But if the word be used in the sense of an appreciation at once cultivated and active, one may say that the formation of taste is the chief matter wherever values enter in, whether intellectual, esthetic or moral. Relatively immediate judgments, which we call tact or to which we give the name of intuition, do not precede reflective inquiry, but are the funded products of much thoughtful experience. Expertness of taste is at once the result and the reward of constant exercise of thinking. Instead of there being no disputing about tastes, they are the one thing worth disputing about, if by "dispute" is signified discussion involving reflective inquiry. Taste, if we use the word in its best sense, is the outcome of experience brought cumulatively to bear on the intelligent appreciation of the real worth of likings and enjoyments. There is nothing in which a person so completely reveals himself as in the things which he judges enjoyable and desirable. Such judgments are the sole alternative to the domination of belief by impulse, chance, blind habit and self-interest. The formation of a cultivated and effectively operative good judgment or taste with respect to what is esthetically admirable, intellectually acceptable and morally approvable is the supreme task set to human beings by the incidents of experience.[41]

If we don't form our tastes intelligently, they will be formed for us:

When theories of values do not afford intellectual assistance in framing ideas and beliefs about values that are adequate to direct action, the gap must be filled by other means. If intelligent method is lacking, prejudice, the pressure of immediate circumstance, self-interest and class-interest, traditional customs, institutions of accidental historic origin, are *not* lacking, and they tend to take the place of intelligence. Thus we are led to our main proposition: *Judgments about values are judgments about the conditions and the results of experienced objects; judgments about that which should regulate the formation of our desires, affections and enjoyments.* For whatever decides their formation will determine the main course of our conduct, personal and social.[42]

This is why Dewey holds that it is so important that the experimental method be employed in the realm of values as well as the realm of ideas:

I do not for a moment suppose that the experiences of the past, personal and social, are of no importance. For without them we should not be able to frame any ideas whatever of the conditions under which objects are enjoyed nor any estimate of the consequences of esteeming and liking them. But past experiences are significant in giving us intellectual instrumentalities of judging just these points. They are tools, not finalities. Reflection upon what we have liked and have enjoyed is a necessity. But it tells us nothing about the *value* of these things until enjoyments are themselves reflectively controlled, or, until, as they are recalled, we form the best judgment possible about what led us to like this sort of thing and what has issued from the fact that we liked it.

We are not, then, to get away from enjoyments experienced in the past and from recall of them, but from the notion that they are the arbiters of things to be further enjoyed. At present, the arbiter is found in the past, although there are many ways of interpreting what in the past is authoritative. Nominally, the most influential conception doubtless is that of a revelation once had or a perfect life once lived. Reliance upon precedent, upon institutions created in the past, especially in law, upon rules of morals that have come to us through unexamined customs, upon uncriticized tradition, are other forms of dependence. It is not for a moment suggested that we can get away from customs and established institutions. A mere break would doubtless result simply in chaos. But there is no danger of such a break. Mankind is too inertly conservative both by constitution and by education to give the idea of this danger actuality. What there is genuine danger of is that the force of new conditions will produce disruption externally and mechanically: this is an ever present danger. The prospect is increased, not mitigated, by the conservatism which insists upon the adequacy of old standards to meet new conditions. What is needed is intelligent examination of the consequences that are actually effected by inherited institutions and customs, in order that there may be intelligent consideration of the ways in which they are to be intentionally modified in behalf of generation of different consequences.

This is the significant meaning of transfer of experimental method from the technical field of physical experience to the wider field of human life.[43]

We wind up our survey of Dewey's pragmatism with his essay on the role of philosophy in the history of civilization, "Philosophy and Civilization." His point is that to understand philosophy *is* to understand its historic function:

It is commonplace that physically and existentially man can but make a superficial and transient scratch upon the outermost rind of the world. It has become a cheap intellectual pastime to contrast the infinitesimal pettiness of man with the vastnesses of the stellar universes. Yet all such comparisons are illicit. We cannot compare existence and meaning; they are disparate. The characteristic life of man is itself the meaning of vast stretches of existences, and without it the latter have no value or significance. There is no common measure of physical existence and conscious experience because the latter is the only measure there is for the former. The significance of being, though not its existence, is the emotion it stirs, the thought it sustains.

It follows that there is no specifiable difference between philosophy and its role in the history of civilization. Discover and define the right characteristic and unique function in civilization, and you have defined philosophy itself.[44]

As had James before him, Dewey finds the life of all thought in its ability to assimilate novel to funded experience:

> Where there is sufficient depth and range of meanings for consciousness to arise at all, there is a function of adjustment, of reconciliation of the ruling interest of the period with preoccupations which had a different origin and an irrelevant meaning. Consider, for example, the uneasy, restless effort of Plato to adapt his new mathematical insights and his political aspirations to the traditional habits of Athens; the almost humorously complacent union of Christian supernaturalism in the middle ages with the naturalism of pagan Greece; the still fermenting effort of the recent age to unite the new science of nature with inherited classic and medieval institutions. The life of all thought is to effect a junction at some point of the new and the old, of deep-sunk customs and unconscious dispositions, that are brought to the light of attention by some conflict with newly emerging directions of activity. Philosophies which emerge at distinctive periods define the larger patterns of continuity which are woven in effecting the enduring junctions of a stubborn past and an insistent future.[45]

Philosophies are therefore seen as vehicles and landmarks of cultural change:

> Philosophy thus sustains the closest connection with the history of culture, with the succession of changes in civilization. It is fed by the streams of tradition, traced at critical moments to their sources in order that the current may receive a new direction; it is fertilized by the ferment of new inventions in industry, new explorations of the globe, new discoveries in science. But philosophy is not just a passive reflex of civilization that persists through changes, and that changes while persisting. It is itself a change; the patterns formed in this junction of the new and the old are prophecies rather than records; they are policies, attempts to forestall subsequent developments. The intellectual registrations which constitute a philosophy are generative just because they are selective and eliminative exaggerations. While purporting to say that such and such is and always *has* been the purport of the record of nature, in effect they proclaim that such and such *should* be the significant value to which mankind should loyally attach itself. Without evidence adduced in its behalf such a statement may seem groundless. But I invite you to examine for yourselves any philosophical idea which has had for any long period a significant career, and find therein your own evidence. Take, for example, the Platonic patterns of cosmic design and harmony; the Aristotelian perpetually recurrent ends and grooved potentialities; the Kantian fixed forms of intellectual synthesis; the conception of nature itself as it figured in seventeenth and eighteenth century thought. Discuss them as revelations of eternal truth, and something almost childlike or something beyond possibility of decision enters in; discuss them as selections from existing culture by means of which to

articulate forces which the author believed should and would dominate the future, and they become preciously significant aspects of human history.[46]

It is because culture is ever-changing that the work of the philosopher, like that of the housekeeper, is never finished. For it consists in "the old and ever new undertaking of adjusting that body of traditions which constitute the actual mind of man to scientific tendencies and political aspirations which are novel and incompatible with received authorities. Philosophers are parts of history, caught in its movement; creators perhaps in some measure of its future, but also assuredly creatures of its past."[47]

CHAPTER SEVEN

Pragmatic Versus Positivistic Empiricism

Twentieth-century Anglo-American philosophy gives great prominence to the study of language. This is in large measure due to the influence of Ludwig Wittgenstein, who, in his *Tractatus Logico-Philosophicus*, contends that the limits of one's language define the limits of one's world. For example, to have a language in which there is no synonym for 'winsome' is to live in a world in which no person (in manner, appearance, smile, etc.) is winsome; to have a language in which there is no subjunctive construction is to live in a world in which there are no lawlike connections; to have a language in which the square root of minus one is never mentioned is to live in a world in which there are no imaginary numbers; and so on. Although we stressed in the last section that John Dewey—as opposed to both Charles Peirce and William James—was a twentieth-century philosopher, one does not find a similar emphasis on language in his writings. In contrast to Wittgenstein who, although he was the paradigmatic twentieth century *philosopher* was in many ways a nineteenth-century *man*, John Dewey was a twentieth-century man although he was in certain ways a nineteenth-century philosopher. And one of those ways was that he produced a philosophy that is not linguicentric in the twentieth-century fashion.

Nevertheless, when Dewey did write about language in the 1920's (for example, in "Nature, Communication and Meaning" [1925]), it was he, not Wittgenstein, who saw this most basic human institution in its proper light. In his "Ontological Relativity" (1968), the latter-day pragmatist W. V. Quine stresses this fact and accounts for it by the naturalism that dominated Dewey's last three decades and that philosophically binds Quine to him:

When a naturalistic philosopher addresses himself to the philosophy of mind, he is apt to talk of language. Meanings are, first and foremost,

79

meanings of language. Language is a social art which we all acquire on the evidence solely of other people's overt behavior under publicly recognizable circumstances. Meanings, therefore, those very models of mental entities, end up as grist for the behaviorist's mill. Dewey was explicit on the point: "Meaning . . . is not a psychic existence; it is primarily a property of behavior."

Once we appreciate the institution of language in these terms, we see that there cannot be, in any useful sense, a private language. This point was stressed by Dewey in the twenties. "Soliloquy," he wrote, "is the product and reflex of converse with others." Further along he expanded the point thus: "Language is specifically a mode of inter-action of at least two beings, a speaker and a hearer; it presupposes an organized group to which these creatures belong, and from whom they have acquired their habits of speech. It is therefore a relationship." Years later, Wittgenstein likewise rejected private language. When Dewey was writing in this naturalistic vein, Wittgenstein still held his copy theory of language.[1]

What Quine is referring to as a "copy theory of language" is simply the attitude toward meaning that is taken by the man on the street and, indeed, has usually been taken by the philosophical tradition:

> Uncritical semantics is the myth of a museum in which the exhibits are meanings and the words are labels. To switch languages is to change the labels. . . .
>
> Seen according to the museum myth, the words and sentences of a language have their determinate meanings. To discover the meanings of a native's words we may have to observe his behavior, but still the meanings of the words are supposed to be determinate in the native's *mind*, his mental museum, even in cases where behavioral criteria are powerless to discover them for us.[2]

Pragmatism has always opposed this myth of a person's mind as a private museum where the meanings of the words he understands are exhibited to him. In particular, there would have been no point in Peirce's pragmatic maxim if the meanings of such words as 'hard,' 'true,' and 'real' could be grasped simply by introspection (a visit to the museum). Remember, these are not esoteric words like 'avulsion' or 'epistasis'; they are words that every child uses with perfect confidence, never dreaming that he does not understand them. So, if the museum myth were correct, we would have no need for a rule for clearly apprehending them. Since the recognition of such a need is of the essence of pragmatism, it is clear that Peirce, Dewey, and their colleagues rejected the myth of the museum.

For Dewey,

1. "Meaning . . . is primarily a property of behavior"[3]

(though secondarily it is a property of the objects referred to by that behavior). "But the behavior of which it is a quality is a distinctive behavior; cooperative, in that response to another's act involves contemporaneous response to a thing as entering into the other's behavior, and this upon both sides."[4] Hence,

2. "Primarily meaning is intent,"[5]

and

3. "Language is . . . a mode of interaction of at least two beings, . . . it presupposes an organized group to which these creatures belong, and from whom they have acquired their habits of speech."[6]

Of the three followers of Dewey we will focus on in this and the next section, W. V. Quine emphasizes the first of these three theses and Donald Davidson and Richard Rorty stress both the second and third.

Quine's "Two Dogmas of Empiricism" was published in January 1951, eighteen months before Dewey died. Alan Donagan, in his 1970 review of *The Encyclopedia of Philosophy*, called it "probably the most influential philosophical paper written since the Second World War."[7] It must have pleased Dewey to have lived to see the banner of pragmatism being born aloft in such strong and capable hands. In 1931, when Quine was a graduate student, he heard Dewey give the first William James Lectures at Harvard (later published as *Art as Experience*). In 1968, it was Quine who gave the first John Dewey Lectures at Columbia: "Ontological Relativity."

Empirical philosophy during the 1930's and 1940's had been dominated by logical positivism, not pragmatism. Indeed, pragmatism had become nearly moribund during those decades. The 1950's and 1960's were a different story. They were dominated by Quine's version of pragmatism: namely, what remains of modern empiricism once it is purified of two dogmas that in large part conditioned it.

One [dogma] is a belief in a fundamental cleavage between truths which are *analytic*, or grounded in meanings independently of matters of fact, and truths which are *synthetic*, or grounded in fact. The other dogma is *reductionism*: the belief that each meaningful statement is equivalent to some logical construct upon terms which refer to immediate experience.[8]

"Two Dogmas of Empiricism" argues that both of these dogmas are ill-founded. These arguments of Quine's tolled the death knell for logical positivism. Why? Because positivism believed the task of philosophy was disclosing and enforcing the precise boundary that separated natural science from speculative metaphysics. Quine's arguments against the analytic-synthetic distinction and reductionism raised serious questions concerning the prior existence of any such boundary and even concerning our ability to draw one in any non-arbitrary fashion. It was the recognition of these consequences of Quine's arguments against the great dogmas of empiricism that produced the shift back toward pragmatism in twentieth-century empiricism. Of course, pragmatism had always been anti-positivistic—remember Peirce's account of why he, James, and their colleagues called their discussion group The Metaphysical Club and James's attack on Clifford's positivism in "The Will to Believe"—but it was Quine's great achievement to be the first to clearly identify the sources of the positivism of Clifford, and kindred spirits.

Quine's attack on the notion of an analytic truth (of a statement that is "true in virtue of meaning") was, in effect, an attack on the notion of meaning itself. For, if we understand what "the *meaning* of t" refers to, for an arbitrary term t, we would know what it means to say that two terms, t_1 and t_2, are synonymous. It would mean that their meanings are identical:

  t_1 and t_2 are *synonymous* if and only if the meaning of t_1 = the meaning of t_2

And, if we understood synonymy, we could use it to explain analyticity:

  A statement is *analytic* if and only if it can be turned into a logical truth by replacing synonyms with synonyms.

For example, if 'squishy' and 'soft' are synonyms, then

  'Whatever is squishy is soft' is analytic,

since

  'Whatever is squishy is squishy' is logically true.

So, in attacking the dogma of the analytic-synthetic distinction, Quine was really calling into question the notion of meaning itself.

Remember that Dewey held that meaning was *primarily* a property of linguistic behavior (or of the expressions that codify that behavior) but *secondarily* a property of the objects referred to by that behavior. If, for example, the meaning of the term 'man' is the property of being a rational animal, then Dewey would also say that this property is, in a secondary sense, *the meaning of* individual men! The traditional term for meaning in this sense is 'essence.' Thus, in Quine's view, Dewey failed to distinguish meaning from essence:

> The Aristotelian notion of essence was the forerunner, no doubt, of the modern notion of intension or meaning. For Aristotle it was essential in men to be rational, accidental to be two-legged. But there is an important difference between this attitude and the doctrine of meaning. From the latter point of view it may indeed be conceded (if only for the sake of argument) that rationality is involved in the meaning of the word 'man' while two-leggedness is not, but two-leggedness may at the same time be viewed as involved in the meaning of 'biped' while rationality is not. Thus from the point of view of the doctrine of meaning it makes no sense to say of the actual individual, who is at once a man and a biped, that his rationality is essential and his two-leggedness accidental or vice versa. Things had essences, for Aristotle, but only linguistic forms have meanings. Meanings is what essence becomes when it is divorced from the object of reference and wedded to the word.[9]

Such a wedding may not produce clarity, but it certainly reduces confusion. When thinking of an actual individual as a mathematician, we are inclined to think of his rationality as essential and his two-leggedness accidental. On the other hand, when thinking of him as a cyclist, it is his two-leggedness that seems essential and his rationality accidental. But what of an actual individual who is both a mathematician and a cyclist? Is this individual essentially rational and accidentally two-legged or vice versa? As Quine points out in another context, just insofar as we are talking referentially of this individual, with no special bias toward a background grouping of mathematicians as against cyclists or vice versa, there is no sense in rating some of his attributes as essential and others as accidental. Some of his attributes count as important and others as unimportant, yes; some as enduring and others as fleeting; but none are essential or accidental. Surely Quine is right about this. Like the bifurcation of substances into those that are quintessential and those that are not, the bifurcation of attributes into those that are essential and those that are not is a piece of archaic metaphysics that has no place in a twentieth-century worldview.

So we will say no more about essences that have not been divorced from the object of reference and wedded to the word. But what about those that have been so divorced and remarried? What about meanings? Once we give up the museum myth, there becomes a question of the extent to which this notion makes sense at all. The crucial fact to bear in mind, Dewey and Quine continue to remind us, is that language is acquired by those who speak it; and, in making that acquisition, the language-learner "has no data to work with but the overt behavior of other speakers."[10] The conclusion that both Dewey and Quine draw from this fact about language-learning is that talk of meaning "is vitiated by a pernicious mentalism as long as we regard a man's semantics as somehow determinate in his mind beyond what might be implicit in his dispositions to overt behavior."[11] As Quine says,

> When with Dewey we turn . . . toward a naturalistic view of language and a behavioral view of meaning, what we give up is not just the museum figure of speech. We give up an assurance of determinacy. . . . When . . . we recognize with Dewey that "meaning . . . is primarily a property of behavior," we recognize that there are no meanings, nor likenesses nor distinctions of meaning, beyond what are implicit in people's dispositions to overt behavior. For naturalism the question whether two expressions are alike or unlike in meaning has no determinate answer, known or unknown, except insofar as the answer is settled in principle by people's speech dispositions, known or unknown. If by these standards there are indeterminate cases, so much the worse for the terminology of meaning and likeness of meaning.[12]

Much of "Ontological Relativity" is devoted to arguing that such indeterminacy of meaning is just what one actually encounters.

Since Quine argues this point in the context of translating an utterly alien language ("radical translation"), his conclusion is usually referred to as *the thesis of the indeterminacy of radical translation*. Suppose, for example, that a field linguist had succeeded in parsing an alien utterance as

1. *Demki gavagai zaronka pursch denot gavagai,*

and had noted that this utterance seemed only to be made on those occasions when, as we would say, a rabbit that had formerly been observed reappeared. Unless such a translation produced conflict with other, equally obvious, ones, the field linguist would no doubt translate 1 as

2. This rabbit is the same as that rabbit,

taking 'rabbit' as the translation of '*gavagai.*' One might think that this translation of '*gavagai*' is a purely objective matter that could be settled by ostension, that is, by pointing to instances. But Quine argues that this is not so. For,

> a whole rabbit is present when and only when an undetached part of a rabbit is present; also when and only when a temporal stage of a rabbit is present. If we are wondering whether to translate a native expression "gavagai" as "rabbit" or as "undetached rabbit part" or as "rabbit stage," we can never settle the matter simply by ostension—that is, simply by repeatedly querying the expression "gavagai" for the native's assent or dissent in the presence of assorted stimulations.[13]

The problem is, as Quine says, that

> "rabbit" is a term of divided reference. As such it cannot be mastered without mastering its principle of individuation: where one rabbit leaves off and another begins. And this cannot be mastered by pure ostension, however persistent.
>
> Such is the quandary over "gavagai": where one gavagai leaves off and another begins. The only difference between rabbits, undetached rabbit parts, and rabbit stages is in their individuation. If you take the total scattered portion of the spatio-temporal world that is made up of rabbits, and that which is made up of undetached rabbit parts, and that which is made up of rabbit stages, you come out with the same scattered portion of the world each of the three times. The only difference is in how you slice it. And how to slice it is what ostension or simple conditioning, however persistently repeated, cannot teach.[14]

Quine's claim is that *'gavagai'* can be translated into English equally defensibly in at least three ways—*viz.* as 'rabbit,' as 'undetached rabbit part,' and as 'rabbit stage.' Note that Quine is not speaking of ambiguity within the alien language. He is supposing that one and the same native use of the expression *'gavagai'* can be given any one of the three English translations, each being accommodated by compensating adjustments in the translation of other words. For example, if *'gavagai'* is translated as 'undetached rabbit part,' then 1 will be translated as

3. This undetached rabbit part is a part of the same rabbit as that undetached rabbit part,

wherein *'zaronka pursch'* is translated as 'is a part of the same rabbit as' rather than as 'is the same as,' as it was translated in 2. Likewise, if *'gavagai'* is translated as 'rabbit stage,' *'zaronka pursch'* will be rendered as 'is a stage of the same rabbit as'; and

4. This rabbit stage is a stage of the same rabbit as that rabbit stage,

rather than either 2 or 3, will be the translation of 1. Quine's point is that, for those who have given up the myth of the museum wherein meanings are exhibited to the introspective consciousness, the question of which of these three translations of *'gavagai'* is correct has no determinate answer, known or unknown:

> Suppose [all three] translations, along with these accommodations in each case, accord equally well with all observable behavior on the part of speakers of the remote language and speakers of English. Suppose they accord perfectly not only with behavior actually observed, but with all dispositions to behavior on the part of all the speakers concerned. On these assumptions it would be forever impossible to know of one of these translations that it was the right one, and the other[s] wrong. Still, if the museum myth were true, there would be a right and wrong of the matter; it is just that we would never know, not having access to the museum. See language naturalistically, on the other hand, and you have to see the notion of likeness of meaning in such a case simply as nonsense.[15]

Of course Quine is fully aware that an actual field linguist would be sensible enough to equate *'gavagai'* with 'rabbit,' dismissing such perverse alternatives as 'undetached rabbit part' and 'rabbit stage':

> This sensible choice and others like it would help in turn to determine his subsequent hypotheses as to what native locutions should answer to the English apparatus of individuation, and thus everything would come out all right. The implicit maxim guiding his choice of "rabbit," and similar choices for other native words, is that an enduring and relatively homogeneous object, moving as a whole against a contrasting background, is a likely reference for a short expression. If he were to become conscious of this maxim, he might celebrate it as one of the linguistic universals, or traits of all languages, and he would have no trouble pointing out its psychological plausibility. But he would be wrong; the maxim is his own imposition, toward settling what is objectively indeterminate. It is a very sensible imposition, and I would recommend no other. But I am making a philosophical point.[16]

Let us be clear about just what that philosophical point is; it is about meaning: If the meaning of a term is what all and only its correct translations share, then the question of what a term means is not an objectively determinate question since the question of which of several nonsynonymous translations of a term is the correct one is itself indeterminate. The indeterminacy of meaning is a consequence of the indeterminacy of translation.

Meaning (or intension) usually stands in sharp contrast to reference (or extension). A concrete general term (like 'rabbit') refers to each, severally, of any number of concrete objects (such as rabbits). The totality of the objects among which such a term divides its reference (for example, the order *Lagomorpha*) is called its extension. The intension of a term means that trait or complex of traits (for example, rabbithood, the property of being lagomorphic) that all and only members of its extension share. Quine has been arguing that this notion of intension is vacuous, that is, that the question of what the intension of a term is does not have a determinate answer. Intension is inscrutable in that there is nothing to scrutinize. What is striking about his argument for this claim is that it applies to extension as well as intension. "At the level of radical translation," Quine argues, "extension itself goes inscrutable":

> It is philosophically interesting, moreover, that what is indeterminate in this artificial example is not just meaning, but extension; reference. My remarks on indeterminacy began as a challenge to likeness of meaning. I had us imagining "an expression that could be translated into English equally defensibly in either of two ways, unlike in meaning in English." Certainly likeness of meaning is a dim notion, repeatedly challenged. Of two predicates which are alike in extension, it has never been clear when to say that they are alike in meaning and when not; it is the old matter of featherless bipeds and rational animals or of equiangular and equilateral triangles. Reference, extension, has been the firm thing; meaning, intension, the infirm. The indeterminacy of translation now confronting us, however, cuts across extension and intension alike. The terms "rabbit," "undetached rabbit part," and "rabbit stage" differ not only in meaning; they are true of different things. Reference itself proves behaviorally inscrutable.
>
> Within the parochial limits of our own language, we can continue as always to find extensional talk clearer than intensional. For the indeterminacy between "rabbit," "rabbit stage," and the rest depended only on a correlative indeterminacy of translation of the English apparatus of individuation—the apparatus of pronouns, pluralization, identity, numerals, and so on. No such indeterminacy obtrudes so long as we think of this apparatus as given and fixed. Given this apparatus, there is no mystery about extension; terms have the same extension when true of the same things. At the level of radical translation, on the other hand, extension itself goes inscrutable.[17]

Given the indeterminacy of the translation of '*gavagai*' into English, what the alien speaker uses that term to refer to is itself behaviorally inscrutable. Perhaps '*gavagai*' is a general term that he predicates of rabbits, but it might also be a general term that he predicates of integral rabbit parts or of temporal stages of rabbits. Indeed, for him, it might not be a general term at all. It might be an abstract singular term that speakers of his language use to refer to rabbithood—in which case the translation of 1 would be

5. This instantiation of rabbithood manifests the same rabbit as that instantiation of rabbithood

or a concrete singular term that the alien uses to refer to the so-called *mereological sum* (or *fusion*) of the order *Lagomorpha*, that is, that single though discontinuous portion of the spatiotemporal world that consists of rabbits—in which case the translation of 1 would be

6. This part of the rabbit-fusion is the same rabbit as that part of the rabbit-fusion

or even a mass term (like 'wood' or 'water') that the alien uses to refer to the world's "rabbit-stuff" (the stuff of which rabbits are composed), in which case

7. This portion of rabbit-stuff is the same rabbit as that portion of rabbit-stuff

would translate 1. Insofar as we cannot say which, if any, of 2–7 is the correct translation of 1 into English, we cannot say whether *'gavagai'* refers to rabbits or their parts, stages, essences, fusion, or stuff. This is the inscrutability of reference.

It is not, Quine argues, the inscrutability of fact: "There is no fact of the matter."[18] The argument is the argument from naturalism:

> Philosophically I am bound to Dewey by the naturalism that dominated his last three decades. With Dewey I hold that knowledge, mind, and meaning are part of the same world that they have to do with, and that they are to be studied in the same empirical spirit that animates natural science. There is no place for a prior philosophy.[19]

The prior philosophy from the vantage point of which philosophers had traditionally viewed language—their "uncritical semantics"—is the so-called "copy theory of language," which Quine sees as a "pernicious mentalism" and which he refers to (with deliberate abusiveness) as "the museum myth." For one who holds a naturalistic view of language, there is no place in his theorizing for such mythological semantics:

Semantics is vitiated by a pernicous mentalism as long as we regard a man's semantics as somehow determinate in his mind beyond what might be implicit in his dispositions to overt behavior. It is the very facts about meaning, not the entities meant, that must be construed in terms of behavior.[20]

And, as we have seen, the same can be said about reference: It is the very facts about reference that must be construed in terms of behavior. For naturalism, the question of whether an alien speaker is using *'gavagai'* to refer to what an English speaker refers to as 'rabbit' has no determinate answer, known or unknown, except insofar as that answer is settled in principle by the alien's and the English speaker's speech dispositions. If by these standards there are indeterminate cases, so much the worse for the terminology of reference and the sameness of reference in the context of radical translation.

If, for example, the claims that the alien speaker uses *'gavagai'* to refer to rabbits and that he uses it to refer to rabbithood accord equally well with all dispositions to behavior on the part of speakers of the alien language and of speakers of English, then it would be forever impossible to know which of these claims is the right one, and which is wrong. Those who see language naturalistically will have to see the notion of reference as nonsense in such a case. If the question of whether the alien speaker is referring to rabbits or rabbithood remains undecided by the totality of human dispositions to verbal behavior, it is indeterminate in principle. And therefore Quine urged "in defense of the behavioral philosophy of language, Dewey's, that the inscrutability of reference is not the inscrutability of a fact; there is no fact of the matter."[21] For naturalism, there is no fact of *any* matter that is indeterminate in principle.

Both this behavioristic semantics and the naturalistic epistemology from which it is derived play crucial roles in "The Pragmatists' Place in Empiricism." There Quine identifies five significant advances in post-Humean empiricism, and considers the views of the classical pragmatists with respect to these "five points when empiricism has taken a turn for the better."[22] I label these five turning points of empiricism:

1. Methodological nominalism
2. Ontological contextualism
3. Epistemological holism
4. Methodological monism
5. Epistemological naturalism

Point 1 is "the policy, in epistemology, of talking about linguistic expressions where possible instead of ideas."[23] According to Quine, it was introduced into empiricism by John Horne Tooke in 1786. Point 2 is the policy of relying on contextual definition in order to be able, in good conscience, to enjoy the services of a convenient but ontologically embarrassing term while disclaiming its denotation. This came to play a dominant role in empiricism with Russell's theory of singular descriptions in 1905, but Quine traces its origins to Jeremy Bentham's theory of fictions (ca. 1815). Point 3 is the recognition "that in a scientific theory even a whole sentence is ordinarily too short a text to serve as an independent vehicle of empirical meaning,"[24] and that only a reasonably inclusive body of scientific theory, taken as a whole, can so serve. This thesis was introduced into empiricism by Pierre Duhem in 1906. Point 4 is Morton White's term for "abandonment of the analytic-synthetic dualism,"[25] which, we have seen, goes back to Quine's classic paper of 1951. Point 5 is "abandonment of the goal of a first philosophy prior to science."[26] It was Quine's *Word and Object* (1960) that reorientated modern empiricism in this direction, but Quine sees its empirical origins in the positive philosophy of Auguste Comte in 1830.

Quine's epistemological naturalism does not force him to regard man as the discoverer, rather than the inventor, of scientific truth in general. That is to say, it does not separate him from the classical pragmatists:

> James's kind words to wishful thinkers reverberated, though, as kind words will. They inspired F.C.S. Schiller. Schiller, with his philosophy of humanism, was Protagoras *redivivus*. But at this point, a funny thing happened. He had a doctrine of "postulation," which had us believing whatever we wish were true until it proves troublesome. Now the funny thing is that this is a fair account of the hypothetico-deductive method—wishful thinking subject to correction. Apart from an indefinable element of fun, this is pretty much what Popper has described as conjecture and refutation. And incidentally, recalling my five steps of post-Humean empiricism, we may note that this postulational or hypothetico-deductive account is already well suited to the holistic or system-centered position.
>
> Popper and the rest of us who celebrate the hypothetico-deductive method, depart from Schiller's humanism, it may be supposed, in thinking of it as a method of finding truth rather than making it. But I cannot agree. Despite my naturalism, I am bound to recognize that the systematic structure of scientific theory is manmade. It is made to fit the data, yes, but invented rather than discovered, because it is not uniquely determined by the data. Alternative systems, all undreamed of, would have fitted the data, too.
>
> The pragmatists James, Schiller, and Dewey viewed science as a conceptual shorthand for organizing observations. Idealists in Europe held the same view: Mach, Pearson, Poincaré, perhaps Ramsey. And now I, for all my vaunted naturalism, seem drawn into the same position. Is there no difference?

The difference is to be sought in ontology. For James and the European idealists that I named reality consisted primarily in sensation. Schiller's reality was a primordially formless substance shaped by the mind of man. Dewey's reality consisted of observable objects. Similarly, it seems, for Mead. For naturalistic philosophers such as I, on the other hand, physical objects are real, right down to the most hypothetical of particles, though this recognition of them is subject, like all science, to correction. I can hold this ontological line of naive and unregenerate realism, and at the same time I can hail man as largely the author rather than discoverer of truth. I can hold both lines because the scientific truth about physical objects is still the *truth*, for all man's authorship. In my naturalism, I recognize no higher truth than that which science provides or seeks. The scientist is indeed creative, he posits the physical objects, and could perhaps have produced a different system that would fit all past and future data just as well; but to say all this is to affirm truths still within science, about science. These truths illuminate the methodology of our science but do not falsify or supersede our science. We make do with what we have and improve it when we see how. We are always talking within our going system when we attribute truth; we cannot talk otherwise. Our system changes, yes. When it does, we do not say that truth changes with it; we say that we had wrongly supposed something true and have learned better. Fallibilism is the watchword, not relativism. Fallibilism and naturalism.[27]

Naturalism in psychology and semantics, Quine tells us, is behaviorism. And this, he finds, is what genuinely links him to the classical pragmatists:

Naturalism can show itself also in fallibilism. If with naturalism you forswear the ideal of a first philosophy, and if, in addition, you forswear analyticity, then fallibilism comes easily. For whatever reason, fallibilism was endemic among the pragmatists. Dewey, White tells us, scotched the quest for certainty. But fallibilism in Peirce and James had a basis unrelated to naturalism. They believed in an element of absolute chance: that the future was uncertain in principle.

Peirce was decidedly naturalistic, however, in repudiating Cartesian doubt. We should recognize that we are born into a going conceptual scheme, he held; and we should work critically within it, doubting when conflicts arise. Peirce scored a major point for naturalism, moreover, in envisioning a behavioristic semantics. Naturalism in psychology and semantics is behaviorism; and Peirce declared for such a semantics when he declared that beliefs consist in dispositions to action.

The doctrine has its attractions. If we were to ascribe beliefs in the light merely of declarations, we would have the question of veracity to reckon with. The behavioral approach by-passes that. Also it by-passes the problem of interpreting the believer's words, which he may mean differently from the way we would mean them. Moreover, if a behavioral theory accommodated beliefs generally, it would explain sentence meanings generally; for as I remarked earlier, the meaning of a sentence could be said to comprise the dispositions to action that would constitute belief in the truth of the sentence.

Any general theory of belief *or* of sentence meanings, along these lines, is of course moonshine—to borrow an epithet from James. Dispositions to behavior are of very limited service as criteria of belief. What behavior manifests my belief that Brutus killed Caesar? We must not include verbal behavior here, or the behavioral doctrine of belief loses its point. Furthermore, even in cases where we can sensibly speak of taking some nonverbal action on the strength of a belief, there is generally no clear way to ascertain the belief from the action; for there will commonly be a complex of contributory beliefs, some supporting others. We can ascertain belief from action in primitive cases, where theory is at a minimum. Elsewhere, action evinces specific beliefs only when generously eked out with verbal testimony.

Evidently Peirce's behavioral account of belief is not one to rest with. There is no hope of carrying it out sentence by sentence. What is laudable about it is just its behaviorist spirit. Peirce made a general and explicit declaration for behaviorism, indeed, in the following terms: "We have no power of Introspection, but all knowledge of the internal world is derived by hypothetical reasoning from our knowledge of external facts." This spirit reappears with new vigor in Mead's philosophy and psychology, and also in Dewey's semantics. Dewey long preceded Wittgenstein in insisting that there is no more to meaning than is to be found in the social use of linguistic forms.[28]

Indeed, Quine concludes his account of the place of pragmatism in modern empiricism as follows:

I could have listed behavioristic semantics as a sixth great step of post-Humean empiricism. I did not do so because I see it as integral to naturalism. Yet Comte, who preached naturalism, stopped short of behavioristic semantics. The credit must go to the pragmatists.

It is significant that Charles Morris, who was a disciple of the pragmatist Mead, chose the word 'pragmatics' for the behavioral end of the study of language. I am encouraged to think that behavioristic semantics is as distinctive a trait of pragmatism as any; and, indeed, Morris has asserted as much. Certainly it is a trait that I applaud. It long since separated me from the logical positivists. But the term 'pragmatism' is of little service as an alternative name for this one trait.

The professing pragmatists do not relate significantly to what I took to be the five turning points in post-Humean empiricism. Tooke's shift from ideas to words, and Bentham's from words to sentences, were not detectable in Peirce's pragmatic maxim, but we found Peirce's further semantic discussions to be sentence-oriented in implicit ways. Peirce seemed at odds with Duhem's system-centered view, until we got to Peirce's theory of truth; but this we found unacceptable. Other pragmatists were sentence-oriented in an implicit way, but still at odds with the system-centered view, until we made hypothetico-deductive sense of Schiller's humanism. On the analytic-synthetic distinction, and on naturalism, the pragmatists blew hot and cold.

Thayer tried to formulate the distinctive tenets of pragmatism, but the result was complex, and to make it come out right he had to pad his roster with some honorary pragmatists. In limiting my attention to the card-carriers, I have found little in the way of shared and distinctive tenets. The two best guesses seemed to be behavioristic semantics, which I so heartily approve, and the doctrine of man as truth-maker, which I share in large measure.[29]

CHAPTER EIGHT

Post-Quinean Pragmatism

We have seen that W. V. Quine is a somewhat reluctant pragmatist. This reluctance is even more pronounced in the writings of Quine's leading disciple, Donald Davidson. All but one of the readings from Davidson have been taken from his book, *Inquiries into Truth and Interpretation*, which is dedicated "To W. V. Quine, without whom not." Davidson concludes his introduction to this book with the following paragraph:

> W. V. Quine was my teacher at a crucial stage in my life. He not only started me thinking about language, but he was the first to give me the idea that there is such a thing as being right, or at least wrong, in philosophy, and that it matters which. Without the inspiration of his writing, his patient tutelage, his friendly wit and his generous encouragement, this book would not be worse than it is. It would not be.[1]

This section of the course might well have been titled "Contemporary Pragmatism." Yet since Donald Davidson writes (to a great extent) in reaction to Quine, and Richard Rorty writes (to a great extent) in reaction to Quine and Davidson, it seems appropriate that a segment of a course devoted to the writings of Davidson and Rorty should bear a title that makes their indebtedness to Quine manifest.

The previous chapter stressed the fact that Quine's revival of pragmatism in 1951 moved empiricism away from logical positivism. Quine says that

> Carnap, [C.I.] Lewis, and others take a pragmatic stand on the question of choosing between language forms, scientific frameworks; but their pragmatism leaves off at the imagined boundary between the analytic and the synthetic. In repudiating such a boundary I espouse a more thorough

pragmatism. Each man is given a scientific heritage plus a continuing
barrage of sensory stimulation; and the considerations which guide him
in warping his scientific heritage to fit his continuing sensory promptings
are, where rational, pragmatic.[2]

There are various ways of viewing Quine's move. In particular, if one
thinks that logical positivism was a revolutionary philosophical movement, the leading edge of a battle to liberate humanity from the
metaphysical and theological shackles that had held them in bondage
for centuries, then the move away from positivism will be seen as a
reactionary movement, a victory for the defenders of metaphysical
flummery over the forces for scientific clarity of mind. Indeed, I am
afraid that it has often been seen in exactly that way. Of course, those
who have taken the study of pragmatism this far are aware that pragmatists
from Peirce ("metaphysics is a subject much more curious than useful,
the knowledge of which, like that of a sunken reef, serves chiefly to
enable us to keep clear of it"[3]) to Quine ("knowledge, mind, and meaning
. . . are to be studied in the same empirical spirit that animates natural
science. There is no place for a prior philosophy."[4]) have been acutely
aware of the metaphysical excesses that mark our intellectual heritage
and have commended the spirit that animates the natural sciences as
mankind's best hope for avoiding such excesses in the future. Nonetheless,
until one comes to see logical positivism somewhat differently than
those educated before the impact of Quine's work was fully grasped, a
conflict will remain.

It is one of Richard Rorty's principal intellectual achievements to have
resolved that conflict for a generation of philosophers. This was accomplished in his book *Philosophy and the Mirror of Nature* (1979). Rorty
there argues that logical positivism and, more generally, the entire "kind
of philosophy which stems from Russell and Frege"[5]—analytic philosophy—was not a revolutionary mode of thought, but a reactionary
movement. It is, Rorty argues,

> like classical Husserlian phenomenology, simply one more attempt to put
> philosophy in the position which Kant wished it to have—that of judging
> other areas of culture on the basis of its special knowledge of the
> "foundations" of these areas. "Analytic" philosophy is one more variant
> of Kantian philosophy, a variant marked principally by thinking of rep-
> resentation as linguistic rather than mental, and of philosophy of language
> rather than "transcendental critique," or psychology as the discipline which
> exhibits the "foundations of knowledge."[6]

The emphasis on language, Rorty argues, although important in itself,
"does not essentially change the Cartesian-Kantian problematic, and thus

does not really give philosophy a new self-image. For analytic philosophy is still committed to the construction of a permanent, neutral framework for inquiry, and thus for all culture."[7] And it is just this idea, the idea that there are "nonhistorical conditions of any possible historical developments,"[8] and the "attempt to escape from history"[9] that it entails that render analytic philosophy a historical irrelevancy. For surely we must recognize that, as Dewey says, philosophers "are parts of history, caught in its movement; creators perhaps in some measure of its future, but also assuredly creatures of its past."[10]

Rorty's essay "The World Well Lost" (1972) puts the Quinean refutation of logical positivism into a larger historical perspective. But this essay revolves around an argument taken from Davidson's classic essay "On the Very Idea of a Conceptual Scheme," (1973) of which Rorty had read an early version before writing "The World Well Lost." As Davidson's title suggests, what is problematic is not so much the idea of *alternative* conceptual schemes, but the idea of a conceptual scheme *per se*. This is Kant's idea of a system of *a priori* concepts or categories; that is, a system of concepts necessary for the constitution (as opposed to the prediction or control) of experience. Were there such a conceptual framework, it would provide non-historical conditions that any possible historical development must satisfy; it would therefore function as a permanent neutral framework for inquiry. Thus, in challenging this distinction between the constituting scheme and the sensory content of our experience, Davidson has joined forces with the great historicist philosophers from Hegel to Dewey. Since Rorty stresses the historicist element in pragmatism, it is not surprising that he argues that "Davidson's attack on this distinction is the best current expression of the pragmatist attempt to break with the philosophical tradition."[11]

Belief in the scheme-content dualism, Davidson contends in "On the Very Idea of a Conceptual Scheme," is another dogma of empiricism, analogous to belief in the analytic-synthetic dualism or belief in reductionism:

> I want to urge that this . . . dualism of scheme and content, of organizing system and something waiting to be organized, cannot be made intelligible and defensible. It is itself a dogma of empiricism, the third dogma. The third, and perhaps the last, for if we give it up it is not clear that there is anything distinctive left to call empiricism.[12]

Each of these three dogmas of empiricism presupposes an ability to make a distinction that is empirically unwarranted. The dogma of reductionism presupposes that we can distinguish the factual component in the truth of a statement from the linguistic component. The dogma of the analytic-synthetic dualism presupposes that we can distinguish which statements are true in virtue of the linguistic component alone, without regard to the factual component. The dogma of the scheme-content dualism presupposes that we can distinguish between changes in our choice of which statements to hold true which result from changes in our conceptual scheme from those which result from change in our grasp of empirical fact.

We can phrase the presupposition of this third dogma of empiricism more succinctly: It is the belief that we can distinguish *changes in statements held true* due to *changes in meaning* from those held true due to *changes in belief*. For example, before the work of Benjamin Franklin, most so-called electricians held true the sentence 'Electricity is a fluid.' After the work of Franklin and his immediate successors, the electricians no longer held this. Was it because the meaning of the word 'electricity' had changed, or because beliefs about electricity had changed? According to Davidson, the assumption that these questions have determinate answers is a dogma of empiricism: Changes in the meaning of 'electricity' would be changes in our conceptual scheme, whereas changes in belief about electricity would be changes in the empirical content that scheme served to organize. Once we give up the dualism of scheme and content, we give up the assumption that we can distinguish changes in meaning from changes in belief. Belief and meaning are interdependent.

It is this fact that poses the problem of interpretation:

The interdependence of belief and meaning springs from the interdependence of two aspects of the interpretation of speech behaviour: the attribution of beliefs and the interpretation of sentences. We remarked before that we can afford to associate conceptual schemes with languages because of these dependencies. Now we can put the point in a somewhat sharper way. Allow that a man's speech cannot be interpreted except by someone who knows a good deal about what the speaker believes (and intends and wants), and that fine distinctions between beliefs are impossible without understood speech; how then are we to interpret speech or intelligibly to attribute beliefs and other attitudes? Clearly we must have a theory that simultaneously accounts for attitudes and interprets speech, and which assumes neither.

I suggest, following Quine, that we may without circularity or unwarranted assumptions accept certain very general attitudes towards sentences as the basic evidence for a theory of radical interpretation. For the sake of the present discussion at least we may depend on the attitude of accepting as true, directed to sentences, as the crucial notion. (A more full-blooded theory would look to other attitudes towards sentences as well, such as wishing true, wondering whether true, intending to make true, and so on.) Attitudes are indeed involved here, but the fact that the main issue is not begged can be seen from this: if we merely know that someone holds a certain sentence to be true, we know neither what he means by the sentence nor what belief his holding it true represents. His holding the sentence true is thus the vector of two forces: the problem of interpretation is to abstract from the evidence a workable theory of meaning and an acceptable theory of belief.[13]

Davidson speaks of "radical interpretation"—a phrase that forms the title of one his most influential essays (1973). Remember that Quine coined the term 'radical translation' for "translation from a remote language on behavioral evidence, unaided by prior dictionaries,"[14] and that he argued for the inscrutability of reference in the context of radical translation. Davidson chose the term 'radical interpretation' to suggest "strong kinship with Quine's 'radical translation.' Kinship is not identity, however, and 'interpretation' in place of 'translation' marks one of the differences: a greater emphasis on the explicitly semantical" in radical interpretation.[15]

Another reason for favoring 'interpretation' over 'translation' is that at least one of the problems that both Quine and Davidson address "is domestic as well as foreign: it surfaces for speakers of the same language in the form of the question, how can it be determined that the language is the same?"[16] Like me, you utter the word 'rabbit'; but how do I know that you don't mean what I would mean by the phrase 'undetached rabbit part'? As Quine says, "The problem at home differs none from radical translation ordinarily so called except in the willfulness of this suspension of homophonic translation."[17] Davidson, using the more apt term to cover the domestic as well as the foreign case, says, "All understanding of the speech of another involves radical interpretation."

I do not think that this pair of reasons would alone have sufficed to bring Davidson to deviate from his teacher's terminology. There is a deeper issue, one concerned with the need for a *theory* of interpretation. Quine, I believe, would have held what Davidson denies, *viz.* that "a method of translation, from the language to be interpreted into the language of the interpreter, is all the theory that is needed."[18] Davidson argues as follows:

> Such a theory would consist in the statement of an effective method for going from an arbitrary sentence of the alien tongue to a sentence of a familiar language; thus it would satisfy the demand for a finitely stated method applicable to any sentence. But I do not think a translation manual is the best form for a theory of interpretation to take.
>
> When interpretation is our aim, a method of translation deals with a wrong topic, a relation between two languages, where what is wanted is an interpretation of one (in another, of course, but that goes without

saying since any theory is in some language). We cannot without confusion count the language used in stating the theory as part of the subject matter of the theory unless we explicitly make it so. In the general case, a theory of translation involves three languages: the object language, the subject language, and the metalanguage (the languages from and into which translation proceeds, and the language of the theory, which says what expressions of the subject language translate which expressions of the object language). And in this general case, we can know which sentences of the subject language translate which sentences of the object language without knowing what any of the sentences of either language mean (in any sense, anyway, that would let someone who understood the theory interpret sentences of the object language). If the subject language happens to be identical with the language of the theory, then someone who understands the theory can no doubt use the translation manual to interpret alien utterances; but this is because he brings to bear two things he knows and that the theory does not state: the fact that the subject language is his own, and his knowledge of how to interpret utterances in his own language.[19]

Davidson is particularly intent on bringing out what is involved in interpreting utterances of one's own language as well as those of alien languages.

He thinks that what is involved is, in effect, construction of a theory of truth for the object language in the subject language:

A satisfactory theory for interpreting the utterances of a language, our own included, will reveal significant semantic structure: the interpretation of utterances of complex sentences will systematically depend on the interpretation of utterances of simpler sentences, for example. Suppose we were to add to a theory of translation a satisfactory theory of interpretation for our own language. Then we would have exactly what we want, but in an unnecessarily bulky form. The translation manual churns out, for each sentence of the language to be translated, a sentence of the translator's language; the theory of interpretation then gives the interpretation of these familiar sentences. Clearly the reference to the home language is superfluous; it is an unneeded intermediary between interpretation and alien idiom. The only expressions a theory of interpretation has to mention are those belonging to the language to be interpreted.

A theory of interpretation for an object language may then be viewed as the result of the merger of a structurally revealing theory of interpretation for a known language, and a system of translation from the unknown language into the known. The merger makes all reference to the known language otiose; when this reference is dropped, what is left is a structurally revealing theory of interpretation for the object language—couched, of course, in familiar words. We have such theories, I suggest, in theories of truth of the kind Tarski first showed how to give.

What characterizes a theory of truth in Tarski's style is that it entails, for every sentence s of the object language, a sentence of the form:

s is true (in the object language) if and only if p.

Instances of the form (which we shall call T-sentences) are obtained by replacing 's' by a canonical description of s, and 'p' by a translation of s. The important undefined semantical notion in the theory is that of *satisfaction* which relates sentences, open or closed, to infinite sequences of objects, which may be taken to belong to the range of the variables of the object language. The axioms, which are finite in number, are of two kinds: some give the conditions under which a sequence satisfies a complex sentence on the basis of the conditions of satisfaction of simpler sentences, others give the conditions under which the simplest (open) sentences are satisfied. Truth is defined for closed sentences in terms of the notion of satisfaction. A recursive theory like this can be turned into an explicit definition along familiar lines, as Tarski shows, provided the language of the theory contains enough set theory; but we shall not be concerned with this extra step.

Further complexities enter if proper names and functional expressions are irreducible features of the object language. A trickier matter concerns indexical devices. Tarski was interested in formalized languages containing no indexical or demonstrative aspects. He could therefore treat sentences as vehicles of truth; the extension of the theory to utterances is in this case trivial. But natural languages are indispensably replete with indexical features, like tense, and so their sentences may vary in truth according to time and speaker. The remedy is to characterize truth for a language relative to a time and a speaker. The extension to utterances is again straightforward.[20]

So much for the form that a theory of radical interpretation will take. Let us now return to a consideration of evidential factors.

We noted earlier that Davidson follows Quine in taking the attitude of *accepting as true*, directed to sentences, as the basic evidence for such a theory. Thus we, as interpreters, begin with the fact that the subject (the person whose utterance is being interpreted) accepts a certain sentence—for example, 'The yawl sailing by is a handsome craft'—as true. But we do not purport to know what the subject means by 'The yawl sailing by is a handsome craft' or what belief his holding this sentence true represents. In effect, we are regarding the subject's holding 'The yawl sailing by is a handsome craft' true as the vector of two forces; and the problem of interpretation is to abstract from this evidence a workable theory of meaning (in the form of a theory of truth) and an acceptable theory of belief:

The way this problem is solved is best appreciated from undramatic examples. If you see a ketch sailing by and your companion says, 'Look at that handsome yawl', you may be faced with a problem of interpretation. One natural possibility is that your friend has mistaken a ketch for a yawl, and has formed a false belief. But if his vision is good and his line of sight favourable it is even more plausible that he does not use the word 'yawl' quite as you do, and has made no mistake at all about the position of the jigger on the passing yacht. We do this sort of off the cuff interpretation all the time, deciding in favour of reinterpretation of words in order to preserve a reasonable theory of belief. As philosophers we are peculiarly tolerant of systematic malapropism, and practised at interpreting the result. The process is that of constructing a viable theory of belief and meaning from sentences held true.

Such examples emphasize the interpretation of anomalous details against a background of common beliefs and a going method of translation. But the principles involved must be the same in less trivial cases. What matter is this: if all we know is what sentences a speaker holds true, and we cannot assume that his language is our own, then we cannot take even a first step towards interpretation without knowing or assuming a great deal about the speaker's beliefs. Since knowledge of beliefs comes only with the ability to interpret words, the only possibility at the start is to assume general agreement on beliefs. We get a first approximation to a finished theory by assigning to sentences of a speaker conditions of truth that actually obtain (in our own opinion) just when the speaker holds those sentences true. The guiding policy is to do this as far as possible, subject to considerations of simplicity, hunches about the effects of social conditioning, and of course our common-sense, or scientific, knowledge of explicable error.

The method is not designed to eliminate disagreement, nor can it; its purpose is to make meaningful disagreement possible, and this depends entirely on a foundation—*some* foundation—in agreement. The agreement may take the form of widespread sharing of sentences held true by speakers of 'the same language', or agreement in the large mediated by a theory of truth contrived by an interpreter for speakers of another language.

Since charity is not an option, but a condition of having a workable theory, it is meaningless to suggest that we might fall into massive error by endorsing it. Until we have successfully established a systematic correlation of sentences held true with sentences held true, there are no mistakes to make. Charity is forced on us; whether we like it or not, if we want to understand others, we must count them right in most matters. If we can produce a theory that reconciles charity and the formal conditions for a theory, we have done all that could be done to ensure communication. Nothing more is possible, and nothing more is needed.[21]

This is a stunning conclusion. Let us be sure that we understand it. Given only that the subject holds true the sentence, 'The yawl sailing by is a handsome craft,' the interpreter has no straightforward way of sorting out the roles of belief and meaning in explaining why he holds it true. It may be because he falsely believes that the passing yacht lacks a small jigger mast stepped abaft the rudder. But it may also be because he does not use the word 'yawl' as the interpreter does: He may mean by 'yawl' what the interpreter means by 'ketch.' If all the interpreter knows is that the subject holds 'The yawl sailing by is a handsome craft' true, and he cannot assume that the subject means by 'yawl' what he does, then the interpreter cannot take even a first step toward interpretation without knowing or assuming a great deal about the subject's beliefs. *Since knowledge of beliefs comes only with the ability to interpret words, the only possibility at the start is to assume general agreement on beliefs.*

Hence, to begin with, the interpreter must assign to sentences to be interpreted conditions of truth that actually obtain (in the interpreter's opinion) just when the subject holds those sentences true. In a word, the interpreter must interpret charitably. In this case, he must consider the possibility that the subject means by 'yawl' what he himself means by 'ketch.' This is an application of what Quine calls the *Principle of Charity:* "Assertions startlingly false on the face of them are likely to turn on hidden differences of language."[22] Since applying this principle in making interpretations is not an option but a condition of having a workable theory of interpretation, it is meaningless to suggest that we might fall into massive error by endorsing it. Charity is forced on us; whether we like it or not, if we want to understand others, we must count them right in most matters. Moreover, the argument that Davidson makes for this stunning conclusion "makes equally for the conclusion that the general outlines of our view of the world are correct; we individually and communally may go plenty wrong, but only on condition that in most large respects we are right. It follows that when we study what our language—any language—requires in the way of overall ontology, we are not just making a tour of our own picture of things: what we take there to be is pretty much what there is."[23]

Before concluding this account of Davidson's views, it will be well to clarify how Rorty, a philosopher who takes those views to be "the best current statement of a pragmatic position," uses the term 'pragmatism.' In the first part of Rorty's "Pragmatism, Relativism, and Irrationalism" (1980), he gives three characterizations of what is meant by the "vague, ambiguous, and overworked word" *pragmatism.*[24] We consider each of these characterizations.

Rorty's *first characterization of pragmatism* is that "it is simply anti-essentialism applied to notions like 'truth,' 'knowledge,' 'language,' 'morality,' and similar objects of philosophical theorizing."[25] Rorty illustrates this by James's definition of "the true" as "what is good in the way of belief."

James's point was that there *is* nothing deeper to be said: truth is not the sort of thing which *has* an essence. More specifically, his point was that it is no use being told that truth is "correspondence to reality." Given a language and a view of what the world is like, one can, to be sure, pair off bits of the language with bits of what one takes the world to be in such a way that the sentences one believes true have internal structures isomorphic to relations between things in the world. When we rap out routine undeliberated reports like "This is water," "That's red," "That's ugly," "That's immoral," our short categorical sentences can easily be thought of as pictures, or as symbols which fit together to make a map. Such reports do indeed pair little bits of language with little bits of the world. Once one gets to negative universal hypotheticals, and the like, such pairing will become messy and *ad hoc*, but perhaps it can be done. James's point was that carrying out this exercise will not enlighten us about why truths are good to believe, or offer any clues as to why or whether our present view of the world is, roughly, the one we should hold. Yet nobody would have asked for a "theory" of truth if they had not wanted answers to these latter questions. Those who want truth to have an essence want knowledge, or rationality, or inquiry, or the relation between thought and its object, to have an essence. Further, they want to be able to use their knowledge of such essences to criticize views they take to be false, and to point the direction of progress toward the discovery of more truths. James thinks these hopes are vain. There are no essences anywhere in the area. There is no wholesale, epistemological way to direct, or criticize, or underwrite, the course of inquiry.

Rather, the pragmatists tell us, it is the vocabulary of practise rather than of theory, of action rather than contemplation, in which one can say something useful about truth. Nobody engages in epistemology or semantics because he wants to know how "This is red" pictures the world. Rather, we want to know in what sense Pasteur's views of disease picture the world accurately and Paracelsus' inaccurately, or what exactly it is that Marx pictured more accurately than Machiavelli. But just here the vocabulary of "picturing" fails us. When we turn from individual sentences to vocabularies and theories, critical terminology naturally shifts from metaphors of isomorphism, symbolism, and mapping to talk of utility, convenience, and likelihood of getting what we want. To say that the parts of properly analyzed true sentences are arranged in a way isomorphic to the parts of the world paired with them sounds plausible if one thinks of a sentence like "Jupiter has moons." It sounds slightly less plausible for "The earth goes round the sun," less still for "There is no such thing as natural motion," and not plausible at all for "The universe is infinite." When we want to praise or blame assertions of the latter sort of sentence, we show how the decision to assert them fits into a whole complex of decisions about what terminology to use, what books to read, what projects to engage in, what life to live. In this respect they resemble such sentences as "Love is the only law" and "History is the story of class struggle." The whole vocabulary of isomorphism, picturing, and mapping is out of place here, as indeed is the notion of being true *of objects*. If we ask what objects these sentences claim to be true of, we get only unhelpful repetitions of the subject terms—"the universe," "the law," "history." Or, even less helpfully, we get talk about "the facts," or "the way the world is." The natural approach to such sentences, Dewey tells us, is not "Do they get it right?", but more like "What would it be like to believe that? What would happen if I did? What would I be committing myself to?" The vocabulary of contemplation, looking, *theoria*, deserts us just when we deal with theory rather than observation, with programming rather than input. When the contemplative mind, isolated from the stimuli of the moment, takes large views, its activity is more like deciding what to *do* than deciding that a representation is accurate. James's dictum about truth says that the vocabulary of practice is uneliminable, that no distinction of kind separates the sciences from the crafts, from moral reflection, or from art.[26]

This brings Rorty to a *second characterization of pragmatism:* "There is no epistemological difference between truth about what ought to be and truth about what is, nor any metaphysical difference between morality and science."[27] For the pragmatist, ethics and physics are equally objective:

For the pragmatist, the pattern of all inquiry—scientific as well as moral— is deliberation concerning the relative attractions of various concrete alternatives. The idea that in science or philosophy we can substitute "method" for deliberation between alternative results of speculation is just wishful thinking. It is like the idea that the morally wise man resolves his dilemmas by consulting his memory of the Idea of the Good, or by looking up the relevant article of the moral law. It is the myth that rationality consists in being constrained by rule. According to this Platonic myth, the life of reason is not the life of Socratic conversation but an illuminated state of consciousness in which one never needs to ask if one has exhausted the possible descriptions of, or explanations for, the situation. One simply arrives at true beliefs by obeying mechanical procedures.

Traditional, Platonic, epistemologically-centered philosophy is the search for such procedures. It is the search for a way in which one can avoid the need for conversation and deliberation and simply tick off the way things are. The idea is to acquire beliefs about interesting and important matters in a way as much like visual perception as possible—by confronting an object and responding to it as programmed. This urge to substitute *theoria* for *phronesis* is what lies behind the attempt to say that "There is no such thing as natural motion" pictures objects in the same way as does "The cat is on the mat." It also lies behind the hope that some arrangement of objects may be found which is pictured by the sentence

"Love is better than hate," and the frustration which ensues when it is
realized that there may be no such objects. The great fallacy of the tradition,
the pragmatists tell us, is to think that the metaphors of vision, correspondence, mapping, picturing, and representation which apply to small,
routine assertions will apply to large and debatable ones. This basic error
begets the notion that where there are no objects to correspond to we
have no hope of rationality, but only taste, passion, and will. When the
pragmatist attacks the notion of truth as accuracy of representation he is
thus attacking the traditional distinctions between reason and desire, reason
and appetite, reason and will. For none of these distinctions make sense
unless reason is thought of on the model of vision, unless we persist in
what Dewey called "the spectator theory of knowledge."

The pragmatist tells us that once we get rid of this model we see that
the Platonic idea of the life of reason is impossible. A life spent representing
objects accurately would be spent recording the results of calculations,
reasoning through sorites, calling off the observable properties of things,
construing cases according to unambiguous criteria, getting things right.
Within what Kuhn calls "normal science," or any similar social context,
one can, indeed, live such a life. But conformity to *social* norms is not
good enough for the Platonist. He wants to be constrained not merely by
the disciplines of the day, but by the ahistorical and nonhuman nature
of reality itself. This impulse takes two forms—the original Platonic strategy
of postulating novel *objects* for treasured propositions to correspond to,
and the Kantian strategy of finding *principles* which are definatory of the
essence of knowledge, or representation, or morality, or rationality. But
this difference is unimportant compared to the common urge to escape
the vocabulary and practices of one's own time and find something
ahistorical and necessary to cling to. It is the urge to answer questions
like "Why believe what I take to be true?" "Why do what I take to be
right?" by appealing to something *more* than the ordinary, retail, detailed,
concrete reasons which have brought one to one's present view. This urge
is common to nineteenth-century idealists and contemporary scientific
realists, to Russell and to Husserl; it is definatory of the Western philosophical tradition, and of the culture for which that tradition speaks. James
and Dewey stand with Nietzsche and Heidegger in asking us to abandon
that tradition, and that culture.[28]

Rorty sums up by offering a *third and final characterization of pragmatism:*
"It is the doctrine that there are no constraints on inquiry save conversational ones—no wholesale constraints derived from the nature of
the objects, or of the mind, or of language, but only those retail constraints
provided by the remarks of our fellow-inquirers."[29] To be a pragmatist
is to give up attempting to ground the solidarity we feel with our fellow
inquirers in objectivity. It is to see that the craving to do so is a confusion:
Objectivity is to be reduced to solidarity, and the only sense in which

the natural sciences are exemplary of objectivity is that they are among our best models of human solidarity:

> The pragmatist tells us that it is useless to hope that objects will constrain us to believe the truth about them, if only they are approached with an unclouded mental eye, or a rigorous method, or a perspicuous language. He wants us to give up the notion that God, or evolution, or some other underwriter of our present world-picture, has programmed us as machines for accurate verbal picturing, and that philosophy brings self-knowledge by letting us read our own program. The only sense in which we are constrained to truth is that, as Peirce suggested, we can make no sense of the notion that the view which can survive all objections might be false. But objections—conversational constraints—cannot be anticipated. There is no method for knowing *when* one has reached the truth, or when one is closer to it than before.
>
> I prefer this third way of characterizing pragmatism because it seems to me to focus on a fundamental choice which confronts the reflective mind: that between accepting the contingent character of starting-points, and attempting to evade this contingency. To accept the contingency of starting-points is to accept our inheritance from, and our conversation with, our fellow-humans as our only source of guidance. To attempt to evade this contingency is to hope to become a properly-programmed machine. This was the hope which Plato thought might be fulfilled at the top of the divided line, when we passed beyond hypotheses. Christians have hoped it might be attained by becoming attuned to the voice of God in the heart, and Cartesians that it might be fulfilled by emptying the mind and seeking the indubitable. Since Kant, philosophers have hoped that it might be fulfilled by finding the a priori structure of any possible inquiry, or language, or form of social life. If we give up this hope, we shall lose what Nietzsche called "metaphysical comfort," but we may gain a renewed sense of community. Our identification with our community— our society, our political tradition, our intellectual heritage—is heightened when we see this community as *ours* rather than *nature's*, *shaped* rather than *found*, one among many which men have made. In the end, the pragmatists tell us, what matters is our loyalty to other human beings clinging together against the dark, not our hope of getting things right. James, in arguing against realists and idealists that "the trail of the human serpent is over all," was reminding us that our glory is in our participation in fallible and transitory human projects, not in our obedience to permanent nonhuman constraints.[30]

With these characterizations of pragmatism in mind, let us consider Davidson's "A Coherence Theory of Truth and Knowledge" (1983) and Rorty's response to it, "Pragmatism, Davidson and Truth" (1986).

Davidson calls his theory of truth and knowledge a "coherence theory." Such theories of truth, at least, are usually advanced in opposition to so-called "correspondence theories," which claim that truth is agreement with reality; that is, that truths are true in virtue of a relationship of correspondence (differently elaborated by different correspondence theories) they bear to some reality (usually said to be a fact). Coherence theories, on the other hand, claim that truth is essentially a system. Those who hold coherence theories of truth characteristically see the progress of knowledge as a progress toward a single, complete system of belief, and they maintain that, strictly speaking, truth is predicable of this system alone. When one remembers that Davidson has argued that theories of meaning are theories of truth and that he takes a holistic view of meaning ("we can give the meaning of any sentence [or word] only by giving the meaning of every sentence [and word] in the language"[31]), it is not surprising that he should favor a coherence theory of truth and knowledge. But one should not jump to the conclusion that his idea of a coherence theory in any way conflicts with his notion of a correspondence theory. In fact, quite the contrary is the case, as he tells us in the opening paragraph of "A Coherence Theory": "In this paper I defend what may as well be called a coherence theory of truth and knowledge. The theory I defend is not in competition with a correspondence theory, but depends for its defense on an argument that purports to show that coherence yields correspondence."[32]

What brings truth and knowledge together, for Davidson, is meaning. This raises a question: If meanings are given by objective truth conditions, how can one ever know that his beliefs satisfy those conditions? The standard correspondence theorist contends that such knowledge requires a confrontation between what we believe and reality; but Davidson admits that "the idea of such a confrontation is absurd."[33] His slogan is *correspondence without confrontation*: "But if coherence is a test of truth, then coherence is a test for judging that objective truth conditions are satisfied, and we no longer need to explain meaning on the basis of possible confrontation."[34] Notice that coherence is spoken of as a *test*, as opposed to a *definition*, of true belief. "It should be clear that I do not hope to define truth in terms of coherence and belief. Truth is beautifully transparent compared to belief and coherence, and I take it as primitive," writes Davidson.[35]

But in precisely what sense can coherence be taken to be a test of true belief? Davidson is not claiming that every belief in a coherent set is true:

> Of course some beliefs are false. Much of the point of the concept of belief is the potential gap it introduces between what is held to be true and what is true. So mere coherence, no matter how strongly coherence is plausibly defined, can not guarantee that what is believed is so. All

that a coherence theory can maintain is that most of the beliefs in a coherent total set of beliefs are true.

This way of stating the position can at best be taken as a hint, since there is probably no useful way to count beliefs, and so no clear meaning to the idea that most of a person's beliefs are true. A somewhat better way to put the point is to say there is a presumption in favor of the truth of a belief that coheres with a significant mass of belief. Every belief in a coherent total set of beliefs is justified in the light of this presumption, much as every intentional action taken by a rational agent (one whose choices, beliefs and desires cohere in the sense of Bayesian decision theory) is justified.[36]

So a coherence theory in Davidson's sense can be taken as an answer to the skeptical question: "Why couldn't all my beliefs hang together and yet be comprehensively false about the actual world?"[37] It is a test of truth only in the sense of providing an answer to this question, that is, of providing "a skeptic with a reason for supposing coherent beliefs are true."[38]

How Davidson accomplishes that is one of the most interesting features of his paper. In calling *all* of our beliefs in question, the skeptic forces those who would answer to do so from a vantage point outside of the set of language-games that form our non-epistemic lives. The problem in responding to skepticism has always been the lack of an outside standpoint. "There is," as Quine writes, "no such cosmic exile."[39] Well, Davidson discovered one: the standpoint of the radical interpreter:

A speaker who wishes his words to be understood cannot systematically deceive his would-be interpreters about when he assents to sentences— that is, holds them true. As a matter of principle, then, meaning, and by its connection with meaning, belief also, are open to public determination. I shall take advantage of this fact in what follows and adopt the stance of a radical interpreter when asking about the nature of belief. What a fully informed interpreter could learn about what a speaker means is all there is to learn; the same goes for what the speaker believes.[40]

This is another instance of the naturalism that Quine celebrates in Peirce and Dewey and passed on to Davidson: What an omniscient or "fully informed" interpreter *could not* learn is indeterminate in principle and *eo ipso* there is nothing to learn, nothing to be skeptical about, "no fact of the matter."

As we have already seen, since the radical interpreter has no choice but to apply the principle of charity in trying to understand a speaker, it is meaningless to suggest that he might fall into massive error by endorsing it: If we want to understand others, we must count them right on most matters:

> It is an artifact of the interpreter's correct interpretation of a person's speech and attitudes that there is a large degree of truth and consistency in the thought and speech of an agent. But this is truth and consistency by the interpreter's standards. Why couldn't it happen that speaker and interpreter understand one another on the basis of shared but erroneous beliefs? This can, and no doubt often does, happen. But it cannot be the rule. For imagine for a moment an interpreter who is omniscient about the world, and about what does and would cause a speaker to assent to any sentence in his (potentially unlimited) repertoire. The omniscient interpreter, using the same method as the fallible interpreter, finds the fallible speaker largely consistent and correct. By his own standards, of course, but since these are objectively correct, the fallible speaker is seen to be largely correct and consistent by objective standards. We may also, if we want, let the omniscient interpreter turn his attention to the fallible interpreter of the fallible speaker. It turns out that the fallible interpreter can be wrong about some things, but not in general; and so he cannot share universal error with the agent he is interpreting. Once we agree to the general method of interpretation I have sketched, it becomes impossible correctly to hold that anyone could be mostly wrong about how things are.[41]

The general method of radical interpretation Davidson has sketched differs from Quine's method of radical interpretation, as we have seen, in various ways. A key difference that we have not yet mentioned plays a crucial role in Davidson's arguments against global skepticism:

> The difference lies in the nature of the choice of causes that govern interpretation. Quine makes interpretation depend on patterns of sensory stimulation, while I make it depend on the external events and objects the sentence is interpreted as being about. Thus Quine's notion of meaning is tied to sensory criteria, something he thinks that can be treated also as evidence. This leads Quine to give epistemic significance to the distinction between observation sentences and others, since observation sentences are supposed, by their direct conditioning to the senses, to have a kind of extra-linguistic justification. This is the view against which I argued in the first part of my paper, urging that sensory stimulations are indeed part of the causal chain that leads to belief, but cannot, without confusion, be considered to be evidence, or a source of justification, for the stimulated beliefs.
>
> What stands in the way of global skepticism of the senses is, in my view, the fact that we must, in the plainest and methodologically most basic cases, take the objects of a belief to be the causes of that belief.

And what we, as interpreters, must take them to be is what they in fact are. Communication begins where causes converge: your utterance means what mine does if belief in its truth is systematically caused by the same events and objects.[42]

The *sine qua non* of a coherence theory, according to Davidson, is "the claim that nothing can count as a reason for holding a belief except another belief."[43] In particular, so-called sensory stimulations cannot so count. Accordingly, Davidson suggests that we "give up the idea that meaning or knowledge is grounded in something that counts as an ultimate source of evidence. No doubt meaning and knowledge depend on experience, and experience ultimately on sensation. But this is the 'depend' of causality, not of evidence or justification."[44] Before turning to Rorty's response to Davidson's coherence theory of truth and knowledge, let us note one barrier to understanding that Davidson sees as particularly prominent:

What I take to be the important aspect of this approach is apt to be missed because the approach reverses our natural way of thinking of communication derived from situations in which understanding has already been secured. Once understanding has been secured we are able, often, to learn what a person believes quite independently of what caused him to believe it. This may lead us to the crucial, indeed fatal, conclusion that we can in general fix what someone means independently of what he believes and independently of what caused the belief. But if I am right, we can't in general first identify beliefs and meanings and then ask what caused them. The causality plays an indispensable role in determining the content of what we say and believe. This is a fact we can be led to recognize by taking up, as we have, the interpreter's point of view.[45]

Whereas the problem of communication is generally one of determining belief given credence and meaning, the problem of interpretation is quite different. It is a matter of determining meaning given credence and belief. Unless we are clear about that, little that Davidson says will make much sense.

Now let us turn to Rorty's "Pragmatism, Davidson and Truth," the essay with which we conclude our study of pragmatism. We have seen that Davidson, in speaking of coherence and correspondence theories of truth, does not intend to explain what truth consists in. Like James and Dewey before him, Davidson rejects the subject-object dualism ("the idea that something like 'mind' or 'language' can bear some relation such as 'fitting' or 'organizing' to the world"[46]) that creates the need for such an explanation of the nature of truth. Like James, Davidson sees 'true' as "a term of praise, a term used for endorsing, rather than one referring to a state of affairs the existence of which explained, e.g., the practical successes of those who held true beliefs."[47] Where Davidson goes beyond James is in seeing that, in addition to

1. an endorsing use,

the truth predicate also has

2. a cautionary use

and

3. a disquotational use,

which James neglected.[48] The cautionary use of 'true' occurs in such remarks as 'I agree that your belief in your partner's honesty is perfectly justified; still, it may not be true.' The disquotational use of 'true' occurs in such remarks as 'If the testimony of the last witness is true, then at least one of the accused is guilty.' Davidson, Rorty argues, "has given us an account of truth which has a place for each of these uses while eschewing the idea that the expediency of a belief can be explained by its truth."[49] *Rather than this account of truth making Davidson an antipragmatist, the argument is to the effect that it makes him the first pragmatist to have given a satisfactory account of truth.* It is Rorty's contention that Davidson can be said to be a pragmatist in virtue of adherence to the following four theses:

1. "True" has no explanatory uses.
2. We understood all there is to know about the relation of beliefs to the world when we understand their causal relations with the world; our knowledge of how to apply terms like "about" and "true of" to sentences is fallout from a "naturalistic" account of linguistic behavior.
3. There are no relations of "being made true" which hold between beliefs and the world.
4. There is no point to debates between realism and anti-realism, for such debates presuppose the empty and misleading idea of beliefs "being made true."[50]

In attributing these four theses to Davidson, Rorty is claiming that he is a pragmatist according to each of the characterizations of pragmatism in "Pragmatism, Relativism, and Irrationalism." In virtue of thesis 1, Davidson would be an antiessentialist with respect to truth. In virtue of theses 2 and 3, he would abjure all epistemological and metaphysical differences between facts and values. And, in virtue of thesis 4, Davidson would be committed to renouncing all constraints on inquiry save conversational ones. So it is clear that Davidson would be a pragmatist (in Rorty's sense of the term, at least) if he held theses 1–4. The greater part of "Pragmatism, Davidson and Truth" is devoted to arguing that Davidson does indeed hold these theses.

The beliefs referred to in 3 are, for Davidson, simply "sentences held true by someone who understands them"[51] and Davidson regards the question 'What makes sentence S true?' as nothing more than a confused version of the question 'What is it for sentence S to be true?' It is confused because it suggests "that truth must be explained in terms of a relation between a sentence as a whole and some entity, perhaps a fact, or state of affairs,"[52] and thus takes us in an utterly wrong direction. In Davidson's view, Tarski's Convention T provides the remedy. It

> shows how to ask the original question without inviting those subsequent formulations. The form of T-sentences already hints that a theory can characterize the property of truth without having to find entities to which sentences that have the property differentially correspond.[53]

It is thus that 3 comes to be a Davidsonian thesis:

> Nothing, . . . no *thing*, makes sentences and theories true: not experience, not surface irritations, not the world, can make a sentence true. *That* experience takes a certain course, that our skin is warmed or punctured, that the universe is finite, these facts, if we like to talk that way, make sentences and theories true. But this point is put better without mention of facts. The sentence 'My skin is warm' is true if and only if my skin is warm. Here there is no reference to a fact, a world, an experience, or a piece of evidence.[54]

Since what holds true for sentences *eo ipso* holds true for sentences held true by someone who understands them, that is, as beliefs, the attribution of thesis 3 to Davidson should not be controversial.

Next, consider thesis 4, that the realism–anti-realism debate is pointless since it presupposes the empty and misleading idea of beliefs "being made true." Since Davidson concluded in "On the Very Idea of a Conceptual Scheme" with the following paragraph he has often been represented as taking the realism side in this debate:

> In giving up dependence on the concept of an uninterpreted reality, something outside all schemes and science, we do not relinquish the notion of objective truth—quite the contrary. Given the dogma of a dualism of

scheme and reality, we get conceptual relativity, and truth relative to a scheme. Without the dogma, this kind of relativity goes by the board. Of course truth of sentences remains relative to language, but that is as objective as can be. In giving up the dualism of scheme and world, we do not give up the world, but reestablish unmediated touch with the familiar objects whose antics make our sentences and opinions true or false.[55]

And Davidson has not been reluctant to accept the epithet. Surely it would be unrealistic to expect otherwise; only those who had lost touch with the familiar objects—the citrus fruits, dry fruits, fruit vegetables, the birds, fish, tables, armchairs, vehicles, machines, and so on—"whose antics make our sentences and opinions true or false"[56] would think of objecting to being called realistic. But to say this indicates nothing about what position such a person would (should) take concerning the debate between professional philosophers who claim that an objective world (one that exists independent of our thought and language) makes our true statements true (the realists) and those who take issue with that claim (the anti-realists). Clearly, when the issue is formulated in this way, Davidson is an anti-realist: We have just seen that he denies that the world makes sentences in general true. How could one be more anti-realistic than that?

By so clearly coming down on both sides of this supposed issue, Davidson is in fact showing that—from his perspective—it is a non-issue. Those who see the question "What makes our beliefs true?" as a confusion will feel as much (and as little) kinship with those who answer "The world" as with those who dispute with them. To such a person, this dispute will present the spectacle, as Kant says, of one man trying to milk a he-goat and another holding a sieve underneath. Since it is difficult to imagine Davidson with either he-goat or sieve in hand, let us concede Rorty's attribution of thesis 4, as well as thesis 3, to Davidson.

Next, consider thesis 2. The naturalistic account of linguistic behavior therein mentioned is the account that a radical interpreter or a field linguist making a radical translation could come up with. In attributing thesis 2 to Davidson, Rorty is claiming that the philosophy of language of such a radical interpreter or field linguist "is all the philosophy of language (and, in particular, all the doctrine about truth) which Davidson has, and all that he thinks anybody needs."[57] That Davidson holds this view is clear. As previously noted, it is simply the Deweyan naturalism that came to him through Quine: "What a fully informed interpreter could learn about what a speaker means is all there is to learn; the same goes for what the speaker believes."[58] So, again, Rorty is justified in attributing the thesis to Davidson. Moreover, the most important parts of "Pragmatism, Davidson and Truth" argue that not only is 2 Davidson's position, it is a position he is justified in maintaining.

So only Rorty's attribution of thesis 1 to Davidson remains to be considered. His claim is that, given Davidson's semantic holism, thesis 1 is a corollary of thesis 2. The argument for this claim is rather involved. We have seen that Davidson holds that utterances are synonymous if beliefs in their truth are systematically caused by the same events and objects ("Communication begins where causes converge"[59]). He came to this view, according to Rorty, by wedding

> the Kripkean claim that causation must have *something* to do with reference to the Strawsonian claim that you figure out what somebody is talking about by figuring out what object most of his beliefs are true of. The wedding is accomplished by saying that Strawson is right if construed holistically—if one prefaces his claim with Aristotle's phrase "on the whole and for the most part". You cannot, however, use Strawson's criterion for individual cases to be sure of being right. But if *most* of the results of your translation-scheme, and consequent assignment of reference, do not conform to Strawson's criterion, then that scheme must have something terribly wrong with it. The mediating element between Strawson and Kripke is the Quinean insight that knowledge *both* of causation *and* of reference is (equally) a matter of coherence with the field linguist's own beliefs.[60]

For the naturalist, there is nothing else for it to be. For, if there were, then there would be a place for a prior philosophy.

Kripke's approach to reference stands in sharp contrast to Davidson's holistic approach. For instance, if thesis 2 were construed in terms of Kripke's atomistic (or "building-block") approach to reference, the idea would be to trace causal pathways from objects to individual speech-arts. According to Rorty:

> This approach leaves open the possibility that speakers may get these pathways all wrong (e.g., by being largely wrong about what there is) and thus that they may never know to what they are referring. This allows the possibility of a wholesale divorce between referents and intentional objects—just the kind of scheme-content gap which Davidson warns us against. But contrast, Davidson is suggesting that we maximize coherence and truth first, and then let reference fall out as it may.[61]

This guarantees that, in the majority of cases, the intentional objects of beliefs will be among their causes. For we must not forget that the Principle of Charity is "not an option, but a condition of having a

workable theory of interpretation."[62] The radical interpreter or field
linguist

> can communicate with the natives if he knows most of their intentional
> objects (i.e., which objects most of their rules for action are good for
> dealing with, which objects most of their beliefs are true of). But he can
> make as little sense of the skeptical claim that this is not "really"
> communication (but just accidentally felicitous cross-talk) as of the sug-
> gestion that the "intended interpretation" of some platitudinous native
> utterance is "There are no rocks."[63]

Pace the skeptic, Rorty agrees with Davidson that there is nothing more
to be known about the relation between beliefs and the rest of reality
than what the radical interpreter or translator can learn from his study
of causal transactions ("prompted assents") between organisms and their
environment.

> The relevant result of this study is the field linguist's translation-manual-
> cum-ethnographic-report. Since we already have (in dictionaries) a trans-
> lation manual for ourselves, as well as (in encyclopedias) an auto-eth-
> nography, there is nothing more for us to know *about our relation to reality*
> than we already know. There is, in this area, no further job for philosophy
> to do. This is just what the pragmatist has been telling the skeptic all the
> time. Both the pragmatist and Davidson are saying that if "correspondence"
> denotes a relation between beliefs and the world which can vary though
> nothing else varies—even if all the causal relations remain the same—
> then "corresponds" cannot be an explanatory term. So if truth is to be
> thought of as "correspondence", then "true" cannot be an explanatory
> term. Pressing (2) to the limit, and freeing it from the atomistic presup-
> positions which Kripkean "building-block" theories of reference add to it,
> results in (1).[64]

Thus Rorty shows that thesis 1 can also be attributed to Davidson.

Having argued that theses 1–4 can all be attributed to Davidson,
Rorty feels justified in claiming that Davidson's philosophical achievements belong to the American pragmatic tradition.

CHAPTER ONE

1. Quoted in Bruce Kuklick, *The Rise of American Philosophy* (New Haven and London: Yale University Press, 1979), p. xv.

2. *Ibid.*

3. *Ibid.*

4. *Philosophical Writings of Peirce*, ed. J. Buchler (New York: Dover Publications, Inc., 1955), p. 252.

5. *Ibid.*

6. C. S. Peirce, *Collected Papers* (Cambridge, Mass.: Harvard University Press, 1932), 2.113.

7. *Philosophical Writings of Peirce*, pp. 1–2.

8. Willis Doney, "Cartesianism," *The Encyclopedia of Philosophy*, ed. Paul Edwards (New York and London: Macmillan Publishing Co. Inc. & The Free Press, 1972), Vol. II, p. 37.

9. *Philosophical Writings of Peirce*, p. 228.

10. W. V. Quine, *Theories and Things* (Cambridge, Mass.: The Belknap Press of Harvard University Press, 1981), p. 68.

11. Richard Rorty, *Philosophy and the Mirror of Nature* (Princeton, N.J.: Princeton University Press, 1980), pp. 48–51. Here Rorty quotes Anthony Kenny, "Descartes on Ideas," in *Descartes: A Collection of Critical Essays*, ed. Willis Doney (Garden City, N.Y.: Doubleday, 1967), p. 226.

12. *Philosophical Writings of Peirce*, p. 228.

13. *Ibid.*, pp. 228–229.

14. *Ibid.*, p. 229.

15. *Ibid.*

16. John Dewey, *Experience and Nature* (New York: Dover Publications, Inc., 1958), p. 3a.

CHAPTER TWO

1. William James Earle, "James, William," *The Encyclopedia of Philosophy*, ed. Paul Edwards (New York and London: Macmillan Publishing Co. Inc. & The Free Press, 1972), Vol. IV, p. 240.

2. Ralph Barton Perry, *The Thought and Character of William James* (Westport, Conn.: Greenwood Press, 1974), Vol. I, p. 211.

3. Bruce Kuklick, *The Rise of American Philosophy* (New Haven and London: Yale University Press, 1979), p. 160.

4. *Ibid.*, p. 47.

5. *Ibid.*, p. 48.

6. *Ibid.*

7. *Ibid.*, p. 47.

8. *Ibid.*, p. 161.

9. "James, William," p. 241.

10. *The Rise of American Philosophy*, p. 160.

11. *The Writings of William James*, ed. John J. McDermott (Chicago and London: The University of Chicago Press, 1977), p. 7.

12. *The Rise of American Philosophy*, p. 168.

13. William James, *The Will to Believe* (New York: Dover Publications, Inc., 1956), pp. 113–114.

14. *The Writings of William James*, pp. 7–8.

15. *The Rise of American Philosophy*, p. 165.

16. *Ibid.*

17. *Ibid.*

18. Henry Steele Commager, *The American Mind* (New Haven: Yale University Press, 1950), pp. 82–83.

19. Jack Kaminsky, "Spencer, Herbert," *The Encyclopedia of Philosophy*, Vol. VIII, p. 523, cited in note 1, above.

20. *The American Mind*, p. 89.

21. *Ibid.*, p. 86.

22. *Ibid.*, p. 87.

23. *Ibid.*, p. 92.

24. *Ibid.*

25. *Ibid.*, p. 88.

26. *Ibid.*, p. 89.

27. *Ibid.*, p. 92.

CHAPTER THREE

1. *Charles S. Peirce: Selected Writings*, ed. Philip Wiener (New York: Dover Publications, Inc., 1966), p. 31.

2. *Philosophical Writings of Peirce*, ed. Justus Buchler (New York: Dover Publications, Inc., 1955), pp. 269–270.

3. *Ibid.*, pp. 9–10.

4. *Ibid.*, p. 10.

5. *Ibid.*, pp. 10–11.

6. *Ibid.*, pp. 26–27.

7. W. Z. Sawrey and J. D. Weisz, "An experimental method of producing gastric ulcers," *Journal of Comparative and Physiological Psychology* 49(1956):269–270.

8. J. V. Brady, R. W. Porter, D. G. Conrad, and J. W. Mason, "Avoidance behavior and the development of gastro-duodenal ulcers," *Journal of Experimental Analysis of Behavior* 1(1958):69–72.

9. *Philosophical Writings of Peirce*, p. 27.

10. *Ibid.*, p. 28.

11. *Ibid.*

12. *Ibid.*

13. *Ibid.*

14. *Ibid.*

15. *Ibid.*, p. 29.

16. *Ibid.*, p. 30.

17. *Ibid.*

18. *Ibid.*, p. 31.

19. *Ibid.*

20. *Ibid.*

21. *Ibid.*, p. 30.

22. *Ibid.*, p. 251.

23. *Ibid.*, p. 18.

24. *Ibid.*, pp. 36–37.

25. *Ibid.*, p. 38.

CHAPTER FOUR

1. Ralph Barton Perry, *The Thought and Character of William James*, (Westport, Conn.: Greenwood Press, 1974), Vol. II, p. 407.

2. H. S. Thayer, "Pragmatism," *The Encyclopedia of Philosophy*, ed. Paul Edwards (New York and London: Macmillan Publishing Co. Inc. & The Free Press, 1972), Vol. VI, p. 431.

3. Henry Steele Commager, *The American Mind* (New Haven: Yale University Press, 1950), p. 91.

4. William James, *The Will to Believe* (New York: Dover Publications, Inc., 1956), p. 64.

5. *Ibid.*

6. *Ibid.*, p. 63.

7. *The Writings of William James*, ed. John J. McDermott (Chicago and London: The University of Chicago Press, 1977), p. 346.

8. *The Will to Believe*, p. 66.

9. *Ibid.*, p. 77.

10. *Ibid.*, p. 82.

11. *Ibid.*, p. 86.

12. *Ibid.*, pp. 163–164.

13. *Philosophical Writings of Peirce*, ed. Justus Buchler (New York: Dover Publications, Inc., 1955), p. 338.

14. *The Writings of William James*, pp. 610–611.

15. *Ibid.*, p. 616.

16. *Ibid.*, p. 623.

17. *Ibid.*, p. 625.

18. Ralph Barton Perry, *The Thought and Character of William James: Briefer Version* (Cambridge, Mass.: Harvard University Press, 1948), p. 208.

19. *The Will to Believe*, p. 8.

20. *Ibid.*

21. *Ibid.*, p. 9.

22. *Ibid.*, p. 11.

23. *The Thought and Character of William James: Briefer Version*, p. 215.

24. Oliver Wendell Holmes, Jr., *The Common Law* (Boston: Little, Brown and Co., 1923), p. 1.

25. Oliver Wendell Holmes, Jr., "The Path of Law," *The Holmes Reader* (New York: Oceana Publications, 1925), p. 59.

26. Quoted in *The American Pragmatists*, ed. M. R. Konvitz and G. Kennedy (Cleveland and New York: Meridian Books of World, 1969), p. 144.

CHAPTER FIVE

1. John Dewey, *Essays in Experimental Logic* (Chicago: University of Chicago Press, 1916), p. 329.

2. Ralph Barton Perry, *The Thought and Character of William James* (Westport, Conn.: Greenwood Press, 1974), Vol. II, p. 480.

3. *Ibid.*

4. *The Writings of William James*, ed. John J. McDermott (Chicago and London: The University of Chicago Press, 1977), p. 348.

5. William James, *Pragmatism* (Indianapolis: Hackett Publishing Co., 1981), p. 26.

6. *Philosophical Writings of Peirce*, ed. Justus Buchler (New York: Dover Publication, Inc., 1955), pp. 252–253.

7. *Ibid.*, p. 252.

8. *The Writings of William James*, p. 348.

9. *Ibid.*

10. *Philosophical Writings of Peirce*, p. 36.

11. *The Writings of William James*, p. 348.

12. *Ibid.*

13. *Pragmatism*, p. 25.

14. *The Writings of William James*, p. 349.

15. *Pragmatism*, p. 27.

16. *The Writings of William James*, p. 360.

17. *Ibid.*

18. *Ibid.*

19. *The Thought and Character of William James*, Vol. II., pp. 466–467.

20. *Ibid.*, pp. 408–409.

21. *Pragmatism*, p. 100.

22. *Ibid.*

23. Soren Kierkegaard, *Concluding Unscientific Postscript* (Princeton, N.J.: Princeton University Press, 1941), p. 178.

24. *Pragmatism*, p. 29.
25. *Ibid.*, p. 30.
26. *The Thought and Character of William James*, Vol. II, p. 444.
27. *Pragmatism*, p. 30.
28. *Ibid.*, p. 92.
29. *Ibid.*, p. 100.
30. *Ibid.*
31. *Ibid.*, p. 101.
32. *Ibid.*, p. 38.
33. *Ibid.*, p. 32.
34. *Ibid.*, p. 92.
35. *Ibid.*, p. 38.
36. *Ibid.*, p. 31.
37. *Ibid.*
38. *Ibid.*, p. 101.
39. *Ibid.*
40. *Ibid.*, p. 104.
41. *Ibid.*, pp. 32–33.
42. *Ibid.*, p. 104.
43. *Pragmatism*, p. 95.
44. *Ibid.*, p. 98.
45. *Ibid.*, p. 92.
46. *Ibid.*, p. 100.
47. *Ibid.*, p. 37.
48. *Ibid.*

CHAPTER SIX

1. Sidney Hook, *John Dewey: An Intellectual Portrait* (Westport, Conn.: Greenwood Press, 1971), p. 16.
2. *Ibid.*, p. 15.
3. Richard J. Bernstein, "Dewey, John," *The Encyclopedia of Philosophy*, ed. Paul Edwards (New York: Macmillan Publishing Co. Inc., 1972), Vol. II, p. 384.
4. *Ibid.*
5. *John Dewey: An Intellectual Portrait*, p. 10.
6. *The Philosophy of John Dewey*, Two Volumes in One, ed. John J. McDermott (Chicago and London: The University of Chicago Press, 1981), p. 8.
7. *John Dewey: An Intellectual Portrait*, p. 13.
8. *The Philosophy of John Dewey*, p. 52.
9. *Ibid.*, pp. 52–53.
10. *Ibid.*, p. 54.
11. John Dewey, *The Quest for Certainty* (New York: Capricorn Books, 1960), pp. 16–17.
12. *The Philosophy of John Dewey*, p. 35.

13. John Dewey and Arthur Bentley, *A Philosophical Correspondence, 1932–1951*, ed. S. Ratner and J. Altman (New Brunswick: Rutgers University Press, 1964), p. 643.

14. William James, *Some Problems of Philosophy* (Cambridge, Mass.: Harvard University Press, 1979), p. 32.

15. "Dewey, John," p. 381.

16. John Dewey, *Art as Experience* (New York: Paragon Books, 1979), p. 46.

17. *Ibid.*

18. *Ibid.*, p. 35.

19. *Ibid.*

20. *Ibid.*

21. *Ibid.*, pp. 42–43.

22. *Ibid.*, p. 37.

23. *Ibid.*, p. 50.

24. *Ibid.*, p. 46.

25. *The Quest for Certainty*, p. 224.

26. *The Philosophy of John Dewey*, p. 242.

27. *Ibid.*

28. John Dewey, *Experience and Nature* (New York: Dover Publications, Inc., 1958), p. 21.

29. *Ibid.*, pp. 4–6.

30. *Ibid.*, p. 6.

31. *Ibid.*, pp. 7–8.

32. *Ibid.*, p. 36.

33. *Ibid.*, pp. 37–38.

34. *The Quest for Certainty*, p. 230.

35. *Ibid.*, p. 229.

36. *Ibid.*, pp. 242–243.

37. *Ibid.*, p. 245.

38. *Ibid.*, pp. 245–246.

39. *Ibid.*, pp. 249–250.

40. *Ibid.*, p. 260.

41. *Ibid.*, p. 262.

42. *Ibid.*, p. 265.

43. *Ibid.*, pp. 272–273.

44. John Dewey, *Philosophy and Civilization* (New York: Capricorn Books, 1963), p. 6.

45. *Ibid.*, p. 7.

46. *Ibid.*, pp. 7–8.

47. *Ibid.*, pp. 3–4.

CHAPTER SEVEN

1. W. V. Quine, *Ontological Relativity and Other Essays* (New York: Columbia University Press, 1969), pp. 26–27.

2. *Ibid.*, pp. 27, 28–29.

3. John Dewey, *Experience and Nature* (New York: Dover Publications, Inc., 1958), p. 179.

4. *Ibid.*

5. *Ibid.,* p. 180.

6. *Ibid.,* p. 185.

7. Alan Donagan, "The Encyclopedia of Philosophy," *The Philosophical Review* (January, 1970), p. 91.

8. W. V. Quine, *From a Logical Point of View,* 2nd ed., rev. (New York: Harper Torchbooks, 1963), p. 20.

9. *Ibid.,* p. 22.

10. *Ontological Relativity and Other Essays,* p. 28.

11. *Ibid.,* p. 27.

12. *Ibid.,* pp. 28–29.

13. *Ibid.,* pp. 30–31.

14. *Ibid.,* pp. 31–32.

15. *Ibid.,* pp. 29–30.

16. *Ibid.,* p. 34.

17. *Ibid.,* pp. 34–35.

18. *Ibid.,* p. 38.

19. *Ibid.,* p. 26.

20. *Ibid.,* p. 27.

21. *Ibid.,* p. 47.

22. *Pragmatism: Its Sources and Prospects,* ed. Robert J. Mulvaney and Philip M. Zeltner (Columbia: University of South Carolina Press, 1981), p. 23.

23. *Ibid.,* p. 24.

24. *Ibid.,* p. 26.

25. *Ibid.,* p. 23.

26. *Ibid.,* pp. 23–24.

27. *Ibid.,* pp. 33–34.

28. *Ibid.,* pp. 35–37.

29. *Ibid.,* p. 37.

CHAPTER EIGHT

1. Donald Davidson, *Inquiries into Truth and Interpretation* (Oxford: Clarendon Press, 1984), p. xx.

2. W. V. Quine, *From a Logical Point of View,* 2nd ed. rev. (New York: Harper Torchbooks, 1963), p. 46.

3. *Philosophical Writings of Peirce,* ed. Justus Buchler (New York: Dover Publications, Inc., 1955), p. 40.

4. W. V. Quine, *Ontological Relativity and Other Essays* (New York and London: Columbia University Press, 1969), p. 26.

5. Richard Rorty, *Philosophy and the Mirror of Nature* (Princeton, N.J.: Princeton University Press, 1980), p. 8.

6. *Ibid.*

7. *Ibid.*

8. *Ibid.*, p. 9.

9. *Ibid.*

10. John Dewey, *Philosophy and Civilization* (New York: Capricorn Books, 1963), p. 4.

11. Richard Rorty, "Philosophy as Science, as Metaphor and as Politics," in *The Institution of Philosophy*, ed. Avner Cohen and Marcello Dascal (La Salle, Ill.: Open Court, 1989) p. 18.

12. *Inquiries into Truth and Interpretation*, p. 189.

13. *Ibid.*, pp. 195–196.

14. *Ontological Relativity and Other Essays*, p. 45.

15. *Inquiries into Truth and Interpretation*, p. 126.

16. *Ibid.*, p. 125.

17. *Ontological Relativity and Other Essays*, p. 47.

18. *Inquiries into Truth and Interpretation*, p. 129.

19. *Ibid.*

20. *Ibid.*, pp. 130–131.

21. *Ibid.*, pp. 196–197.

22. *Ibid.*, p. xvii, quoting Quine.

23. *Ibid.*, pp. xviii–xix.

24. Richard Rorty, *Consequences of Pragmatism* (Minneapolis: University of Minnesota Press, 1982), p. 160.

25. *Ibid.*, p. 162.

26. *Ibid.*, pp. 162–163.

27. *Ibid.*, p. 163.

28. *Ibid.*, pp. 164–165.

29. *Ibid.*, p. 165.

30. *Ibid.*, pp. 165–166.

31. *Inquiries into Truth and Interpretation*, p. 22.

32. Donald Davidson, "A Coherence Theory of Truth and Knowledge," *Truth and Interpretation: Perspectives on the Philosophy of Donald Davidson*, ed. Ernest LePore (Oxford and New York: Blackwell, 1986), p. 307.

33. *Ibid.*

34. *Ibid.*

35. *Ibid.*, p. 308.

36. *Ibid.*

37. *Ibid.*, p. 309.

38. *Ibid.*, pp. 309–310.

39. W. V. Quine, *Word and Object* (Cambridge, Mass.: The M.I.T. Press, 1979), p. 275.

40. "A Coherence Theory of Truth and Knowledge," p. 315.

41. *Ibid.*, p. 317.

42. *Ibid.*, pp. 317–318.

43. *Ibid.*, p. 310.

44. *Ibid.*, p. 313–314.

45. *Ibid.*, p. 317.

46. Richard Rorty, "Pragmatism, Davidson and Truth," *Truth and Interpretation* ed. Ernest Le Pore (Oxford and New York: Basil Blackwell, 1986), p. 333.

47. *Ibid.*, p. 334.

48. *Ibid.*, p. 335.

49. *Ibid.*

50. *Ibid.*

51. "A Coherence Theory of Truth and Knowledge," p. 308.

52. *Inquiries into Truth and Interpretation*, p. 70.

53. *Ibid.*

54. *Ibid.*, p. 194.

55. *Ibid.*, p. 198.

56. *Ibid.*

57. "Pragmatism, Davidson and Truth," p. 339.

58. "A Coherence Theory of Truth and Knowledge," p. 315.

59. *Ibid.*, p. 318.

60. "Pragmatism, Davidson and Truth," p. 340.

61. *Ibid.*

62. *Inquiries into Truth and Interpretation*, p. 197.

63. "Pragmatism, Davidson and Truth," p. 341.

64. *Ibid.*, pp. 341–342.

A. READINGS

The following are the readings chosen by Professor Murphy to accompany each of the sections of the text. Concerning the sections with relatively greater reading, Professor Murphy wrote, "It is not suggested that all of the papers in this section should be covered in the lectures for any one semester." Selections not covered in lecture can function "as outside reading and for paper and exam topics."

1. Charles Peirce's Rejection of Cartesianism

1. René Descartes, "Selections from *Meditations on First Philosophy*" (1641). Available in many editions, for example: trans. Donald A. Cress (Indianapolis: Hackett, 1979). Professor Murphy did not specify which selections from this work he had in mind.

2. C. S. Peirce, "Questions Concerning Certain Faculties Claimed for Man" (1868). In:

Charles S. Peirce: Selected Writings, ed. Philip P. Wiener (New York: Dover, 1966), pp. 15–38.
Collected Papers (Cambridge, Mass.: Harvard University Press, 1934), 5.213–5.263.
Writings of Charles S. Peirce: A Chronological Edition (Bloomington: Indiana University Press, 1984), Vol. 2, pp. 193–211.

3. C. S. Peirce, "Some Consequences of Four Incapacities" (1868). In:

Philosophical Writings of Peirce, ed. Justus Buchler (New York: Dover, 1955), pp. 228–250.
Collected Papers, 5.264–5.317.
Writings of Peirce: Chronological, Vol. 2, pp. 211–242.
Charles S. Peirce: Selected Writings, Wiener, pp. 39–72.

2. William James's Teleological Theory of Mind

1. Herbert Spencer, "Life and Mind as Correspondence" (1870), in *The Works of Herbert Spencer*, Vol. 4: *The Principles of Psychology*, Vol. 1 (Osnabruck: Otto Zeller, 1966), pp. 291–294.

2. John Fiske, "Selection from *Outlines of Cosmic Philosophy*" (1874). Fiske's *Outlines of Cosmic Philosophy* (Boston: Houghton, Mifflin and Co., 1902) is four volumes. Professor Murphy did not identify which selections he had in mind. An article-length selection is in *Philosophy in America*, ed. Paul R. Anderson and Max H. Fisch (New York: D. Appleton-Century Co., 1939), pp. 398–412.

3. William James, "Remarks on Spencer's Definition of Mind" (1878). In:

Essays in Philosophy (The Works of William James) (Cambridge, Mass.: Harvard University Press, 1978), pp. 7–22.
Collected Essays and Reviews, ed. Ralph Barton Perry (New York: Longmans, Green, and Co., 1920), pp. 43–68.

3. Peircean Pragmatism

1. Alexander Bain, "Belief" (1868), in *Mental and Moral Science* (London: Longmans, Green, and Co., 1868), pp. 371–385.

2. C. S. Peirce, "The Fixation of Belief" (1877). In:

Philosophical Writings of Peirce, ed. Justus Buchler (New York: Dover, 1955), pp. 5–22.
Collected Papers (Cambridge, Mass.: Harvard University Press, 1934), 5.358–5.387.
Writings of Charles S. Peirce: A Chronological Edition (Bloomington: Indiana University Press, 1986), Vol. 3, pp. 242–257.
Charles S. Peirce: Selected Writings, ed. Philip P. Wiener (New York: Dover, 1966), pp. 91–112.
The American Pragmatists, ed. M. R. Konvitz and G. Kennedy (Cleveland: Meridian Books of World, 1969), pp. 82–99.
Pragmatism: The Classic Writings, ed. H. S. Thayer (Indianapolis: Hackett, 1982), pp. 61–78.
Classic American Philosophers, ed. Max H. Fisch (Englewood Cliffs, N.J.: Prentice-Hall, 1951), pp. 54–70.
American Philosophy in the Twentieth Century, ed. Paul Kurtz (New York: Macmillan, 1966), pp. 47–61.
The Golden Age of American Philosophy, ed. Charles Frankel (New York: George Braziller, 1960), pp. 53–67.

3. C. S. Peirce, "How to Make Our Ideas Clear" (1878). In:

Writings of Peirce, Buchler, pp. 23–41.
Collected Papers, 5.388–5.410.

Writings of Peirce: Chronological, Vol. 3, pp. 257–276.
Peirce: Selected Writings, Wiener, pp. 113–136.
American Pragmatists, Konvitz and Kennedy, pp. 99–118.
Pragmatism: Classic Writings, Thayer, pp. 79–100.
Classic American Philosophers, Fisch, pp. 70–87.
American Philosophy in the Twentieth Century, Kurtz, pp. 62–78.
The Golden Age of American Philosophy, Frankel, pp. 68–80.

4. Inchoate Pragmatism

1. William James, "The Sentiment of Rationality" (1879). In:

The Will to Believe (New York: Dover, 1956), pp. 63–110.
The Will to Believe (The Works of William James) (Cambridge, Mass.: Harvard University Press, 1979), pp. 57–89.
The Writings of William James, ed. John J. McDermott (New York: Random House, 1967), pp. 317–345.
The Golden Age of American Philosophy, ed. Charles Frankel (New York: George Braziller, 1960), pp. 116–143.

2. William James, "The Dilemma of Determinism" (1884). In:

The Will to Believe (Dover), pp. 145–183.
The Will to Believe (Harvard University Press), pp. 114–140.
The Writings of William James, McDermott, pp. 587–610.
The Golden Age of American Philosophy, Frankel, pp. 143–165.

3. William James, "The Moral Philosopher and the Moral Life" (1891). In:

The Will to Believe (Dover), pp. 184–215.
The Will to Believe (Harvard University Press), pp. 141–162.
The Writings of William James, McDermott, pp. 610–629.
Classic American Philosophers, ed. Max H. Fisch (Englewood Cliffs, N.J.: Prentice-Hall, 1951), pp. 165–180.

4. C. S. Peirce, "The Doctrine of Necessity Examined" (1892). In:

Philosophical Writings of Peirce, ed. Justus Buchler (New York: Dover, 1955), pp. 324–338.
Collected Papers (Cambridge, Mass.: Harvard University Press, 1935), 6.35–6.65.
Charles S. Peirce: Selected Writings, ed. Philip P. Wiener (New York: Dover, 1966), pp. 160–179.
The American Pragmatists, ed. M. R. Konvitz and G. Kennedy (Cleveland: Meridian Books of World, 1969), pp. 127–142.
Classic American Philosophers, Fisch, pp. 100–113.
American Philosophy in the Twentieth Century, ed. Paul Kurtz (New York: Macmillan, 1966), pp. 88–100.

5. William James, "The Will to Believe" (1896). In:

The Will to Believe (Dover), pp. 1–31.
The Will to Believe (Harvard University Press), pp. 13–33.
The Writings of William James, McDermott, pp. 717–735.
Pragmatism: The Classic Writings, ed. H. S. Thayer (Indianapolis: Hackett, 1982) pp. 186–208.
Classic American Philosophers, Fisch, pp. 136–148.
American Philosophy in the Twentieth Century, Kurtz, pp. 133–141.

6. Oliver Wendell Holmes, Jr. "The Path of the Law" (1897). In:

The Holmes Reader, ed. Julius J. Marke (New York: Oceana, 1955), pp. 59–85.
The American Pragmatists, Konvitz and Kennedy, pp. 144–166.

5. Jamesian Pragmatism

1. William James, "Philosophical Conceptions and Practical Results" (1898). In:

The Writings of William James, ed. John J. McDermott (New York: Random House, 1967), pp. 345–362.
Pragmatism (Cambridge, Mass.: Harvard University Press, 1975), pp. 257–270.
American Philosophy in the Twentieth Century, ed. Paul Kurtz (New York: Macmillan, 1966), pp. 105–117.

2. William James, *Pragmatism* (Indianapolis: Hackett, 1981). In:

Pragmatism and *The Meaning of Truth* (Cambridge, Mass.: Harvard University Press, 1978).
Writings: 1902–1910 (Library of America; 38), ed. Bruce Kuklick (New York: Literary Classics of the United States, 1987), pp. 479–624.
The Writings of William James, McDermott, pp. 362–443, 449–472.

6. Deweyan Pragmatism

1. John Dewey, "Escape from Peril" (1929). In:

The Quest for Certainty (New York: Capricorn Books, 1960), pp. 3–25.
The Later Works, Vol. 4: 1929 (Carbondale: Southern Illinois University Press, 1984), pp. 3–20.
The Philosophy of John Dewey, Two Volumes in One, ed. John J. McDermott (Chicago: The University of Chicago Press, 1981), pp. 355–371.

2. John Dewey, "The Influence of Darwinism on Philosophy" (1909). In:

Philosophy of Dewey, McDermott, pp. 31–41.
The Middle Works, Vol. 4: 1907–1909, (1977), pp. 3–14.
The Influence of Darwin on Philosophy and Other Essays on Contemporary Thought (New York: Henry Holt and Co., 1910), pp. 1–19.
Classic American Philosophers, ed. Max H. Fisch (Englewood Cliffs, N.J.: Prentice-Hall, 1951), pp. 336–344.

American Thought Before 1900, ed. Paul Kurtz (New York, Macmillan, 1960), pp. 428–437.

3. John Dewey, "The Development of American Pragmatism" (1925). In:

Philosophy of Dewey, McDermott, pp. 41–58.
The Later Works, Vol. 2: 1925–1927, pp. 3–21.
Philosophy and Civilization (New York: Capricorn Books, 1963), pp. 13–35.
Pragmatism: The Classic Writings, ed. H. S. Thayer (Indianapolis: Hackett, 1982), pp. 23–40.

4. John Dewey, "Having an Experience" (1934). In:

Art as Experience (New York: Paragon Books, 1979), pp. 35–57.
The Later Works, Vol. 10: 1934, pp. 42–63.
Philosophy of Dewey, McDermott, pp. 554–573.

5. John Dewey, "The Postulate of Immediate Empiricism" (1905). In:

The Philosophy of Dewey, McDermott, pp. 240–248.
The Middle Works, Vol. 3: 1903–1906, pp. 158–167.
The Influence of Darwin on Philosophy, pp. 226–241.

6. John Dewey, "Experience and Philosophic Method" (1929). In:

Experience and Nature (New York: Dover, 1958), pp. 1–39.
The Later Works, Vol. 1: 1925, pp. 10–41.
Philosophy of Dewey, McDermott, pp. 249–277.

7. John Dewey, "The Supremacy of Method" (1929). In:

Quest for Certainty, pp. 223–253.
The Later Works, Vol. 4: 1929, pp. 178–202.
The American Pragmatists, ed. M. R. Konvitz and G. Kennedy (Cleveland: Meridian Books of World, 1969), pp. 183–200.
Classic American Philosophers, Fisch, pp. 344–360.

8. John Dewey, "The Construction of Good" (1929). In:

Quest for Certainty, pp. 254–286.
The Later Works, Vol. 4: 1929, pp. 203–228.
Philosophy of Dewey, McDermott, pp. 575–598.
The American Pragmatists, Konvitz and Kennedy, pp. 201–225.
Pragmatism: The Classic Writings, Thayer, pp. 290–315.
Classic American Philosophers, Fisch, pp. 360–381.

9. John Dewey, "Philosophy and Civilization" (1927). In:

Philosophy and Civilization, pp. 3–12.
The Later Works, Vol. 3: 1927–1928, pp. 3–10.

The American Pragmatists, Konvitz and Kennedy, pp. 175–182.

7. Pragmatic Versus Positivistic Empiricism

1. John Dewey, "Nature, Communication and Meaning" (1925). In:

Experience and Nature (New York: Dover, 1958), pp. 166–207.
The Later Works, Vol. 1: 1925 (Carbondale: Southern Illinois University Press, 1981), pp. 132–161.

2. W. V. Quine, "Two Dogmas of Empiricism" (1951), in *From a Logical Point of View*, 2nd ed., rev. (New York: Harper Torchbooks, 1963), pp. 20–46.

3. W. V. Quine, "Ontological Relativity" (1968), in *Ontological Relativity and Other Essays* (New York: Columbia University Press, 1969), pp. 26–68.

4. W. V. Quine, "The Pragmatists' Place in Empiricism" (1981), in *Pragmatism: Its Sources and Prospects*, ed. Robert J. Mulvaney and Philip M. Zeltner (Columbia: University of South Carolina Press, 1981), pp. 21–39.

8. Post-Quinean Pragmatism

1. Richard Rorty, "World Well Lost" (1972), in *Consequences of Pragmatism* (Minneapolis: University of Minnesota Press, 1982), pp. 3–18.

2. Donald Davidson, "On the Very Idea of a Conceptual Scheme" (1974), in *Inquiries into Truth and Interpretation* (Oxford: Clarendon Press, 1984), pp. 183–198.

3. Donald Davidson, "Radical Interpretation" (1973), in *Inquiries into Truth and Interpretation*, pp. 125–140.

4. Richard Rorty, "Dewey's Metaphysics" (1977), in *Consequences of Pragmatism*, pp. 72–89.

5. Richard Rorty, "Pragmatism, Relativism, and Irrationalism" (1980), in *Consequences of Pragmatism*, pp. 160–175.

6. Donald Davidson, "A Coherence Theory of Truth and Knowledge" (1983). In:

Kant oder Hegel? ed. Dieter Henrich (Stuttgart, West Germany: Klett-Cotta, 1983), pp. 423ff.
Truth and Interpretation: Perspectives on the Philosophy of Donald Davidson, ed. Ernest LePore (Oxford: Basil Blackwell, 1986), pp. 307–319.

7. Richard Rorty, "Pragmatism, Davidson and Truth" (1986), in *Truth and Interpretation: Perspectives on Davidson*, pp. 333–368.

B. PRIMARY SOURCES

Charles Sanders Peirce

Since its appearance, the standard source for Peirce's writings has been: Charles S. Peirce, *Collected Papers*. The first six volumes were edited by Charles Hartshorne and Paul Weiss, and volumes 7 and 8 were edited by Arthur W. Burks (Cambridge, Mass.: Harvard University Press, 1931–1958).

Vol. 1: *Principles of Philosophy*. 1931.
Vol. 2: *Elements of Logic*. 1932.
Vol. 3: *Exact Logic*. 1933.
Vol. 4: *The Simplest Mathematics*. 1933.
Vol. 5: *Pragmatism and Pragmaticism*. 1934.
Vol. 6: *Scientific Metaphysics*. 1935.
Vol. 7: *Science and Philosophy*. 1958.
Vol. 8: *Reviews, Correspondence, and Bibliography*. 1958.

A more thorough (though still partial) collection of Peirce's published and unpublished writings is: Charles S. Peirce, *Writings of Charles S. Peirce: A Chronological Edition*, edited by Edward C. Moore, Max H. Fisch, and Christian J. Kloesel (Bloomington: Indiana University Press, 1982–   ). This series is projected to comprise twenty volumes; so far only the first three have appeared:

Vol. 1: 1857–1866. 1982.
Vol. 2: 1867–1871. 1984.
Vol. 3: 1872–1878. 1986.

Single volume selections of the Peirce writings most pertinent to pragmatism include:

Philosophical Writings of Peirce, edited and with an introduction by Justus Buchler (New York: Dover, 1955); 28 selections; 412 pp.
Charles S. Peirce: Selected Writings, edited and with an introduction and notes by Philip P. Wiener (New York: Dover, 1966); twenty-nine selections including five not found in *Collected Papers*; 470 pp.

William James

The Works of William James, edited by Frederick H. Burkhardt, Fredson Bowers, and Ignas K. Skrupskelis (Cambridge, Mass.: Harvard University Press, 1975–1988) constitutes a definitive edition of all of James's published and unpublished writings except his letters. This series comprises seventeen titles, each including a new introduction, extensive notes, appendixes, and editorial apparatus.

Pragmatism. 1975.
The Meaning of Truth. 1975.
Essays in Radical Empiricism. 1976.
A Pluralistic Universe. 1977.
Essays in Philosophy. 1978.

The Will to Believe. 1979.
Some Problems of Philosophy. 1979.
The Principles of Psychology. 3 vols. 1981.
Essays in Religion and Morality. 1982.
Talks to Teachers on Psychology. 1983.
Essays in Psychology. 1983.
Psychology: Briefer Course. 1984.
Varieties of Religious Experience. 1985.
Essays in Psychical Research. 1986.
Essays, Comments, and Reviews. 1987.
Manuscript Essays and Notes. 1988.
Manuscript Lectures. 1988.

Harvard University Press has released a paperbound edition combining both the *Pragmatism* and *The Meaning of Truth* texts from their *Works of William James* series. The paperbound includes the notes and omits editorial apparatus and appendixes (which, in the hardbound *Pragmatism*, include James's "Philosophical Conceptions and Practical Results").
Single volume selections of the writings of James include:

The Writings of William James, edited and with an introduction by John J. McDermott (New York: Random House, 1967); includes about sixty essays, including all of those that constitute *Pragmatism* and selections from each of James's other major books. 906 pp.

William James, *Writings: 1902–1910* (Library of America; 38), edited and with notes by Bruce Kuklick (New York: Literary Classics of the United States, 1987), includes *The Varieties of Religious Experience, Pragmatism, A Pluralistic Universe, The Meaning of Truth, Some Problems of Philosophy,* and twenty essays from the 1902–1910 period. 1381 pp.

John Dewey

The Early Works, 1882–1898, The Middle Works, 1899–1924, and *The Later Works, 1925–1953,* edited by Jo Ann Boydston (Carbondale: Southern Illinois University Press, 1967–   ) together constitute a definitive edition of all of Dewey's published writings except his letters. These series will comprise thirty-six volumes, each including a new introduction, notes, appendixes, and editorial apparatus. Paperbound editions omitting the apparatus are available for most of these volumes.

The Early Works, 1882–1898

Vol. 1: 1882–1888. Essays and *Leibniz's New Essays Concerning the Human Understanding.* 1969.
Vol. 2: 1887. *Psychology.* 1967.
Vol. 3: 1889–1892. Essays and *Outlines of a Critical Theory of Ethics.* 1969.
Vol. 4: 1893–1894. Essays and *The Study of Ethics, A Syllabus.* 1971.
Vol. 5: 1895–1898. Essays. 1972.

The Middle Works, 1899–1924

Vol. 1: 1899–1901. Essays, *The School and Society*, and *The Educational Situation*. 1976.
Vol. 2: 1902–1903. Essays, *Studies in Logical Theory*, and *The Child and the Curriculum*. 1976.
Vol. 3: 1903–1906. Essays. 1977.
Vol. 4: 1907–1909. Essays, *The Pragmatic Movement of Contemporary Thought: A Syllabus*, and *Moral Principles in Education*. 1977.
Vol. 5: 1908. *Ethics* (with James H. Tufts). 1978.
Vol. 6: 1910–1911. Essays and *How We Think*. 1978.
Vol. 7: 1912–1914. Essays and encyclopedia articles. 1979.
Vol. 8: 1915. Essays, *German Philosophy and Politics*, and *Schools of Tomorrow*. 1979.
Vol. 9: 1916. *Democracy and Education*. 1980.
Vol. 10: 1916–1917. Essays. 1980.
Vol. 11: 1918–1919. Essays on China, Japan, and the war. 1982.
Vol. 12: 1920. Essays and *Reconstruction in Philosophy*. 1982.
Vol. 13: 1921–1922. Essays. 1983.
Vol. 14: 1922. *Human Nature and Conduct*. 1983.
Vol. 15: 1923–1924. Essays. 1983.

The Later Works, 1925–1953

Vol. 1: 1925. *Experience and Nature*. 1981.
Vol. 2: 1925–1927. Essays and *The Public and Its Problems*. 1984.
Vol. 3: 1927–1928. Essays. 1984.
Vol. 4: 1929. *The Quest for Certainty*. 1984.
Vol. 5: 1929–1930. Essays, *The Sources of a Science of Education, Construction and Criticism*, and *Individualism, Old and New*. 1984.
Vol. 6: 1931–1932. Essays. 1985.
Vol. 7: 1932. *Ethics*, new edition (with James H. Tufts). 1985.
Vol. 8: 1933. Essays and *How We Think*, new edition. 1985.
Vol. 9: 1933–1934. Essays and *A Common Faith*. 1986.
Vol. 10: 1934. *Art as Experience*. 1987.
Vol. 11: 1935–1937. Essays and *Liberalism and Social Action*. 1987.
Vol. 12: 1938. *Logic: The Theory of Inquiry*. 1986.
Vol. 13: 1938–1939. *Experience and Education, Freedom and Culture*, and *Theory of Valuation*. 1988.
Vol. 14: 1939. Essays. 1988.
Vol. 15: 1942–1948. Essays and *Problems of Men*. Forthcoming.
Vol. 16: 1949–1952. Essays and *Knowing and the Known* (with Arthur Bentley). Forthcoming.
The Philosophy of John Dewey, Two Volumes in One, edited and with an introduction and brief commentary to each of the selections by John J. McDermott (Chicago: The University Press of Chicago, 1981) collects forty-four representative Dewey essays. 723 pp.

Willard van Orman Quine

Quine's books include:

A System of Logistic. Cambridge, Mass.: Harvard University Press, 1934.
Mathematical Logic. Rev. ed. Cambridge, Mass.: Harvard University Press, 1951.
Word and Object. Cambridge, Mass.: The M.I.T. Press, 1960.
From a Logical Point of View. 2nd ed., rev. New York: Harper Torchbooks, 1963.
Selected Logic Papers. New York: Random House, 1966.
Set Theory and Its Logic. Rev. ed. Cambridge, Mass.: Belknap Press of Harvard University Press, 1969.
Ontological Relativity and Other Essays. New York: Columbia University Press, 1969.
The Roots of Reference. LaSalle, Ill.: Open Court, 1973.
The Ways of Paradox and Other Essays. Rev. and enlarged ed. Cambridge, Mass.: Harvard University Press, 1976.
The Web of Belief (with J. S. Ullian). 2nd ed. New York: Random House, 1978.
The Time of My Life: An Autobiography. Cambridge, Mass.: The M.I.T. Press, 1980.
Elementary Logic. Rev. ed. Cambridge, Mass.: Harvard University Press, 1981.
Theories and Things. Cambridge, Mass.: Harvard University Press, 1981.
Methods of Logic. 4th ed. Cambridge, Mass.: Harvard University Press, 1982.
Philosophy of Logic. 2nd ed. Cambridge, Mass.: Harvard University Press, 1986.
Quiddities: An Intermittently Philosophical Dictionary. Cambridge, Mass.: Belknap Press of Harvard University Press, 1987.

Richard Rorty

Rorty's books include:

Philosophy and the Mirror of Nature. Princeton: Princeton University Press, 1979.
Consequences of Pragmatism. Minneapolis: University of Minnesota Press, 1982.
Contingency, Irony and Solidarity. Cambridge: Cambridge University Press, 1989.
Objectivity, Relativism and Truth: Philosophical Papers I. Cambridge: Cambridge University Press, forthcoming.
Essays on Heidegger and Others: Philosophical Papers II. Cambridge: Cambridge University Press, forthcoming.

Donald Davidson

Davidson's books include the early work (with Patrick Suppes and Sidney Siegel), *Decision-Making: An Experimental Approach* (Stanford: Stanford University Press, 1957), and two volumes collecting his essays:

Essays on Actions and Events. Oxford: Clarendon Press, 1985.
Inquiries into Truth and Interpretation. Oxford: Clarendon Press, 1985.

The following essays, written by Davidson after these collections appeared, will be of particular interest to students of pragmatism:

"A Coherence Theory of Truth and Knowledge." In *Truth and Interpretation: Perspectives on the Philosophy of Donald Davidson*, ed. Ernest LePore (Oxford: Basil Blackwell, 1986), pp. 307–319.

"A Nice Derangement of Epitaphs." In *Truth and Interpretation: Perspectives*, LePore, pp. 433–446.

"The Myth of the Subjective." In *Relativism: Interpretation and Confrontation*, ed. Michael Krausz (Notre Dame: University of Notre Dame Press, 1989), pp. 159–172.

"The Structure and Content of Truth," *Journal of Philosophy*, June 1990.

C. SECONDARY AND RELATED WORKS

Pragmatism and American Philosophy

Anderson, Paul R., and Max H. Fisch, eds. *Philosophy in America: From the Puritans to James*. New York: D. Appleton-Century Co., 1939.

Aune, Bruce A. *Rationalism, Empiricism, and Pragmaticism: An Introduction*. New York: McGraw-Hill, 1970.

Ayer, A. J. *Origins of Pragmatism: Studies in the Philosophy of Charles Sanders Peirce and William James*. San Francisco: Freeman Cooper, 1968.

————. *American Thought in Transition: The Impact of Evolutionary Naturalism*. Chicago: Rand McNally, 1969.

Caws, Peter, ed. *Two Centuries of Philosophy in America*. Oxford: Basil Blackwell, 1980.

Clarke, D. S., Jr. *Rational Acceptance and Purpose: An Outline of Pragmatist Epistemology*. Lanham, Md.: Rowman and Littlefield, 1989.

Cohen, Morris. *American Thought: A Critical Sketch*. Glencoe, Ill.: Free Press, 1954.

Commager, Henry Steele. *The American Mind: An Interpretation of American Thought and Character Since the 1880's*. New Haven: Yale University Press, 1950.

Conkin, Paul K. *Puritans and Pragmatists: Eight Eminent American Thinkers*. New York: Dodd, Mead, 1968.

Eames, S. Morris. *Pragmatic Naturalism: An Introduction*. Carbondale: Southern Illinois University Press, 1977.

Fisch, Max H., ed. *Classic American Philosophers*. Englewood Cliffs, N.J.: Prentice-Hall, 1951.

Flower, Elizabeth, and Murray G. Murphey. *A History of Philosophy in America*. 2 vols. New York: Capricorn Books, 1977.

Frankel, Charles, ed. *The Golden Age of American Philosophy*. New York: George Braziller, 1960.

Goetzmann, William H., ed. *The American Hegelians*. New York: Alfred A. Knopf, 1973.

Hartshorne, Charles. *Creativity in American Philosophy*. Albany: State University of New York Press, 1984.

Hollinger, David. *In the American Province: Studies in the History and Historiography of Ideas*. Bloomington: Indiana University Press, 1985.

Hollinger, David, and Charles Cupper. *The American Intellectual Tradition, Vol. 2: 1865 to the Present*. New York: Oxford University Press, 1989.

Holmes, Oliver Wendell. *The Common Law*. Edited by Mark DeWolfe Howe. Boston: Little, Brown and Co., 1963.

Hook, Sidney. *The Metaphysics of Pragmatism*. Chicago: Open Court, 1927.

―――. *Pragmatism and the Tragic Sense of Life*. New York: Basic Books, 1974.

Kallen, Horace M. *Indecency and the Seven Arts and Other Adventures of a Pragmatist in Aesthetics*. New York: A.M.S. Press, 1930.

Kallen, Horace M., and Sidney Hook, eds. *American Philosophy Today and Tomorrow*. Salem, N.H.: Ayer Co., 1968.

Kennedy, Gail. *Pragmatism and American Culture*. Boston: Heath, 1950.

Kolenda, Konstantin, ed. *Person and Community in American Philosophy*. Houston: Rice University Press, 1981.

Konvitz, Milton R., and Gail Kennedy, eds. *The American Pragmatists*. Cleveland: Meridian Books of World, 1969.

Kuklick, Bruce. *The Rise of American Philosophy*. New Haven: Yale University Press, 1977.

Kurtz, Paul, ed. *American Thought Before 1900*. New York: Macmillan, 1960.

―――, ed. *American Philosophy in the Twentieth Century*. New York: Macmillan, 1966.

Lewis, J. David, and Richard L. Smith. *American Sociology and Pragmatism: Mead, Chicago Sociology and Symbolic Interaction*. Chicago: University of Chicago Press, 1981.

McDermott, John J. *The Culture of Experience*. New York: New York University Press, 1976.

MacKinnon, Barbara, ed. *American Philosophy: An Historical Anthology*. Albany: State University of New York Press, 1985.

Marcell, David. *Progress and Pragmatism: James, Dewey, Beard and the American Idea of Progress*. Westport, Conn.: Greenwood Press, 1974.

Margolis, Joseph. *Pragmatism Without Foundations: Reconciling Realism and Relativism*. Oxford: Basil Blackwell, 1986.

Marke, Julius J., ed. *The Holmes Reader*. New York: Oceana, 1955.

Marr, David. *American Worlds Since Emerson*. Amherst: University of Massachusetts Press, 1988.

Martland, Thomas R. *The Metaphysics of William James and John Dewey: Process and Structure in Philosophy and Religion*. New York: Philosophical Library, 1963.

Mills, C. W. *Sociology and Pragmatism*. Irving L. Horowitz, ed. New York: Oxford University Press, 1969.

Moore, Edward C. *American Pragmatism: Peirce, James, and Dewey*. Westport, Conn.: Greenwood Press, 1985.

Morris, Charles W. *The Pragmatic Movement in American Philosophy*. New York: George Braziller, 1970.

Morris, Van C., and Young Pai. *Philosophy and the American School*. 2nd ed. Boston: Houghton Mifflin, 1976.

Mulvaney, Robert J., and Philip M. Zeltner, eds. *Pragmatism: Its Sources and Prospects*. Columbia, S.C.: University of South Carolina Press, 1981.

Murray, D. L. *Pragmatism*. New York: Dodge, 1910.

Myers, Gerald, ed. *The Spirit of American Philosophy*. New York: G. P. Putnam's Sons, 1970.

Persons, Stow. *American Minds: A History of Ideas*. Huntington, N.Y.: R. E. Krieger, 1975.

Pratt, James Bissett. *What Is Pragmatism?* New York: Macmillan, 1915.

Riley, Woodbridge I. *American Thought from Puritanism to Pragmatism*. New York: Henry Holt and Co., 1915.

Rorty, Amelie, ed. *Pragmatic Philosophy: An Anthology*. Garden City, N.Y.: Anchor Books, 1966.

Rosenthal, Sandra B. *Speculative Pragmatism*. Amherst: University of Massachusetts Press, 1986.

Rucker, Darnell. *The Chicago Pragmatists*. Minneapolis: University of Minnesota Press, 1969.

Scheffler, Israel. *Four Pragmatists: A Critical Introduction to Peirce, James, Mead, and Dewey*. New York: Routledge, Chapman, and Hall, 1986.

Schneider, Herbert W. *History of American Philosophy*. 2nd ed. New York: Columbia University Press, 1963.

_____ . *Sources of Contemporary Realism in America*. New York: Irvington, 1964.

Shahan, Robert W., and Kenneth R. Merrill, eds. *American Philosophy: From Edwards to Quine*. Norman: University of Oklahoma Press, 1977.

Sheldon, Wilman H. *America's Progressive Philosophy*. New Haven, Conn.: Yale University Press, 1942.

Singer, Marcus G., ed. *American Philosophy*. Cambridge: Cambridge University Press, 1986.

Smith, John E. *The Spirit of American Philosophy*. New York: Oxford University Press, 1963.

_____ . *Purpose and Thought: The Meaning of Pragmatism*. Chicago: University of Chicago Press, 1984.

Stuhr, John J., ed. *Classical American Philosophy: Essential Readings and Interpretive Essays*. New York: Oxford University Press, 1987.

Thayer, H. S. *Meaning and Action: A Critical History of Pragmatism*. Indianapolis: Hackett, 1981.

_____ , ed. *Pragmatism: The Classic Writings*. Indianapolis: Hackett, 1982.

Van Wesep, Hendrikus Boeve. *Seven Sages: The Story of American Philosophy: Franklin, Emerson, James, Dewey, Santayana, Peirce, Whitehead*. New York: Longmans, Green, 1960.

Weinstein, Michael A. *The Wilderness and the City: American Classical Philosophy as a Moral Quest*. Amherst: University of Massachusetts Press, 1982.

Werkmeister, W. H. *A History of Philosophical Ideas in America*. Westport, Conn.: Greenwood Press, 1981.

West, Cornel. *The Evasion of Philosophy: A Genealogy of Pragmatism*. Madison: University of Wisconsin Press, 1989.

White, Morton G. *Toward Reunion in Philosophy*. Cambridge, Mass.: Harvard University Press, 1956.

———. *Documents in the History of American Philosophy: From Jonathan Edwards to John Dewey.* New York: Oxford University Press, 1972.

———, ed. *Science and Sentiment in America: Philosophical Thought from Jonathan Edwards to John Dewey.* New York: Oxford University Press, 1972.

———. *Pragmatism and the American Mind: Essays and Reviews in Philosophy and Intellectual History.* New York: Oxford University Press, 1973.

———. *Social Thought in America: The Revolt Against Formalism.* London: Oxford University Press, 1976.

Wiener, Philip P. *Evolution and the Founders of Pragmatism.* Cambridge, Mass.: Harvard University Press, 1949.

Winetrout, Kenneth. *F.C.S. Schiller and the Dimensions of Pragmatism.* Columbus: Ohio State University Press, 1967.

Zoll, Daniel A. *The Twentieth Century Mind: Essays on Contemporary Thought.* Baton Rouge: Louisiana State University Press, 1967.

Critiques of Pragmatism

Cornforth, Maurice Campbell. *In Defense of Philosophy: Against Positivism and Pragmatism.* London: Lawrence and Wishart, 1950.

Lovejoy, Arthur O. *The Thirteen Pragmatisms, and Other Essays.* Baltimore: Johns Hopkins Press, 1963.

Moore, Adison W. *Pragmatism and its Critics.* Chicago: University of Chicago Press, 1910.

Novak, George. *Pragmatism Versus Marxism: An Appraisal of John Dewey's Philosophy.* New York: Pathfinder Press, 1975.

Prado, C. G. *The Limits of Pragmatism.* Atlantic Highland, N.J.: Humanities Press International, 1987.

Charles Sanders Peirce

Almeder, Robert F. *The Philosophy of Charles S. Peirce: A Critical Introduction.* Oxford: Basil Blackwell, 1980.

Apel, Karl-Otto. *Charles Sanders Peirce: From Pragmatism to Pragmaticism.* Trans. John M. Krois. Amherst: University of Massachusetts Press, 1981.

Bernstein, Richard, ed. *Perspectives on Peirce: Critical Essays on Charles Sanders Peirce.* Westport, Conn.: Greenwood Press, 1980.

Buchler, Justus. *Charles Peirce's Empiricism.* New York: Octagon Books, 1966.

Davis, William. *Peirce's Epistemology.* The Hague: Martinus Nijhoff, 1972.

Esposito, Joseph L. *Evolutionary Metaphysics: The Development of Peirce's Theory of Categories.* Athens: Ohio University Press, 1980.

Fann, K. T. *Peirce's Theory of Abduction.* The Hague: Martinus Nijhoff, 1970.

Feibleman, James K. *An Introduction to Peirce's Philosophy,* New York: Harper and Bros., 1946.

Fisch, Max H. *Peirce, Semeiotic, and Pragmatism.* Bloomington: Indiana University Press, 1986.

Freeman, Eugene, ed. *The Relevance of Charles Peirce.* LaSalle, Ill.: Hegeler Institute, 1983.

Gallie, W. B. *Peirce and Pragmatism*. Westport, Conn.: Greenwood Press, 1975.
Goudge, Thomas A. *The Thought of C. S. Peirce*. New York: Dover, 1969.
Hookway, Christopher. *Peirce*. New York: Routledge, Chapman and Hall, 1985.
Knight, Thomas Stanley. *Charles Peirce*. New York: Twayne, 1965.
Murphey, Murray G. *The Development of Peirce's Philosophy*. Cambridge: Harvard University Press, 1961.
Potter, Vincent G. *Charles S. Peirce on Norms and Ideals*. Amherst: University of Massachusetts Press, 1967.
Reilly, Francis E. *Charles Peirce's Theory of Scientific Method*. New York: Fordham University Press, 1970.
Rescher, Nicholas. *Peirce's Philosophy of Science: Critical Studies in his Theory of Induction and Scientific Method*. Notre Dame: University of Notre Dame Press, 1978.
Skagestad, Peter. *The Road of Inquiry: Charles Peirce's Pragmatic Realism*. New York: Columbia University Press, 1981.
Thompson, Manley. *The Pragmatic Philosophy of C. S. Peirce*. Chicago: University of Chicago Press, 1953.
Wiener, Philip, and Frederic Young, eds. *Studies in the Philosophy of Charles Sanders Peirce*. Cambridge, Mass.: Harvard University Press, 1952.

William James

Allen, Gay W. *William James: A Biography*. New York: The Viking Press, 1967.
──── . *William James*. Minneapolis: University of Minnesota Press, 1970.
Barzun, Jacques. *A Stroll with William James*. Chicago: University of Chicago Press, 1984.
Bird, Graham. *William James*. New York: Routledge, Chapman and Hall, 1987.
Bixler, Julius S. *Religion in the Philosophy of William James*. New York: A.M.S. Press, 1926.
Bjork, Daniel W. *William James: The Center of his Vision*. New York: Columbia University Press, 1988.
Brennan, Bernard P. *The Ethics of William James*. New York: Bookman Associates, 1961.
──── . *William James*. New York: Twayne, 1968.
Corti, W., ed. *The Philosophy of William James*. Hamburg: Felix Meiner Verlag, 1976.
Dooley, Patrick K. *Pragmatism as Humanism: The Philosophy of William James*. Chicago: Nelson-Hall, 1974.
Ford, Marcus P. *The Philosophy of William James: A New Perspective*. Amherst: University of Massachusetts Press, 1982.
James, Henry, Jr., ed. *Letters of William James*. 2 vols. Boston: Little, Brown and Co., 1920.
Levinson, Henry S. *The Religious Investigations of William James*. Chapel Hill: University of North Carolina Press, 1981.
Matthiesen, F. O. *The James Family*. New York: Alfred A. Knopf, 1947.
Moore, Edward C. *William James*. New York: Washington Square Press, 1965.

Myers, Gerald E. *William James: His Life and Thought*. New Haven: Yale University Press, 1986.

Perry, Ralph Barton. *The Thought and Character of William James*. 2 vols. Boston: Little, Brown, and Co., 1935.

————. *The Thought and Character of William James: Briefer Version*. New York: George Braziller, 1954.

————. *In the Spirit of William James*. Westport, Conn.: Greenwood Press, 1979.

Reck, Andrew. *Introduction to William James: An Essay and Selected Texts*. Bloomington: Indiana University Press, 1967.

Roth, John K. *Freedom and the Moral Life: The Ethics of William James*. Philadelphia: Westminster Press, 1969.

Seigfried, Charlene H. *Chaos and Content: A Study in William James*. Athens: Ohio University Press, 1978.

Suckiel, Ellen K. *The Pragmatic Philosophy of William James*. Notre Dame: University of Notre Dame Press, 1985.

Wild, John Daniel. *The Radical Empiricism of William James*. Westport, Conn.: Greenwood Press, 1980.

John Dewey

Alexander, Thomas, M. *John Dewey's Theory of Art, Experience, and Nature: The Horizons of Feeling*. Albany: State University of New York, 1987.

Bernstein, Richard J. *John Dewey*. Atascadero, Calif.: Ridgeview, 1981.

Blewett, John, ed. *John Dewey: His Thought and Influence*. New York: Fordham University Press, 1960.

Boisvert, Raymond D. *Dewey's Metaphysics*. New York: Fordham University Press, 1988.

Boydston, Jo Ann. *Guide to the Works of John Dewey*. Carbondale: Southern Illinois University Press, 1970.

Bullert, Gary. *The Politics of John Dewey*. Buffalo: Prometheus Books, 1983.

Cahn, Steven, ed. *New Studies in the Philosophy of John Dewey*. Hanover, N.H.: University Press of New England, 1977.

Campbell, Harry M. *John Dewey*. New York: Twayne, 1971.

Coughlan, Neil. *Young John Dewey*. Chicago: University of Chicago Press, 1973.

Cruz, Feodor F. *John Dewey's Theory of Community*. New York: P. Lang, 1987.

Damico, Alfonso J. *Individuality and Community: The Social and Political Thought of John Dewey*. Gainesville: University of Florida Presses, 1978.

Dewey, Robert E. *The Philosophy of John Dewey: A Critical Exposition of His Method*. The Hague: Martinus Nijhoff, 1977.

Dicker, Georges. *Dewey's Theory of Knowing*. Philadelphia: University City Science Center, 1976.

Dykhuzien, George. *The Life and Mind of John Dewey*. Carbondale: Southern Illinois University Press, 1973.

Geiger, George R. *John Dewey in Perspective: A Reassessment*. Westport, Conn.: Greenwood Press, 1976.

Gouinlock, James. *John Dewey's Philosophy of Value*. New York: Humanities Press, 1972.

Hendel, Charles W., ed. *John Dewey and the Experimental Spirit in Philosophy*. New York: Liberal Arts Press, 1959.

Hook, Sidney. *John Dewey: An Intellectual Portrait*. Westport, Conn.: Greenwood Press, 1971.

———, ed. *John Dewey: Philosopher of Science and Freedom: A Symposium*. Westport, Conn.: Greenwood Press, 1976.

Kastenbaum, Victor. *The Phenomenological Sense of John Dewey: Habit and Meaning*. Atlantic Highlands, N.J.: Humanities Press, 1977.

Morgenbesser, Sidney, ed. *Dewey and His Critics*. New York: The Journal of Philosophy, 1977.

Nathanson, Jerome. *John Dewey: The Reconstruction of the Democratic Life*. New York: Scribner, 1951.

Peters, R. S., ed. *John Dewey Reconsidered*. London: Routledge and Kegan Paul, 1977.

Ratner, Sidney, Jules Altman, and James E. Wheeler, eds. *John Dewey and Arthur F. Bentley: A Philosophical Correspondence, 1932–1951*. New Brunswick: Rutgers University Press, 1964.

Roth, Robert J. *John Dewey and Self-Realization*. Westport, Conn.: Greenwood Press, 1978.

Schilpp, Paul A., ed. *The Philosophy of John Dewey*. Evanston, Ill.: Northwestern University Press, 1939.

Sleeper, R. W. *The Necessity of Pragmatism: John Dewey's Conception of Philosophy*. New Haven, Conn.: Yale University Press, 1986.

Somjee, A. H. *The Political Theory of John Dewey*. New York: Teachers College Press, 1968.

Thayer, H. S. *The Logic of Pragmatism: An Examination of John Dewey's Logic*. Westport, Conn.: Greenwood Press, 1970.

Tiles, J. E. *Dewey*. New York: Routledge, Chapman and Hall, 1989.

White, Morton G. *The Origins of Dewey's Instrumentalism*. New York: Columbia University Press, 1943.

Zeltner, Philip M. *John Dewey's Aesthetic Philosophy*. Amsterdam: B. R. Gruner, 1975.

Willard van Orman Quine

Barrett, Robert B., and Roger F. Gibson, eds. *Perspectives on Quine*. Oxford: Basil Blackwell, 1989.

Davidson, Donald, and Jaakko Hintikka, eds. *Words and Objections: Essays on the Work of W. V. Quine*. Rev. ed. Dordrecht, Holland: D. Reidel, 1975.

Dilman, Ilham. *Quine on Ontology, Necessity and Experience*. Albany: State University of New York Press, 1984.

Feleppa, Robert. *Convention, Translation, and Understanding: Philosophical Problem in the Comparative Study of Culture*. Albany: State University of New York Press, 1988.

Gibson, Roger F. *The Philosophy of W. V. Quine: An Expository Essay*. Tampa: University of Florida Presses, 1982.

———. *Enlightened Empiricism: An Examination of W. V. Quine's Theory of Knowledge.* Tampa: University of Florida Presses, 1988.

Hahn, Lewis E., and Paul A. Schilpp, eds. *The Philosophy of W. V. Quine.* LaSalle, Ill.: Open Court, 1986.

Heal, Jane. *Normativity and Holism.* Oxford: Basil Blackwell, 1988.

Hookway, Christopher. *Quine: Language, Experience, and Reality.* Stanford: Stanford University Press, 1988.

Ornstein, Alex. *Willard Van Orman Quine.* Boston: Twayne, 1977.

Romanos, George D. *Quine and Analytic Philosophy.* Cambridge, Mass.: The M.I.T. Press, 1983.

Shahan, Robert W., and Chris Swoyer, eds. *Essays on the Philosophy of W. V. Quine.* Norman: University of Oklahoma Press, 1979.

Donald Davidson

LePore, Ernest, ed. *Truth and Interpretation: Perspectives on the Philosophy of Donald Davidson.* Oxford: Basil Blackwell, 1986.

LePore, Ernest, and Brian T. McLaughlin, eds. *Actions and Events: Perspectives on the Philosophy of Donald Davidson.* Oxford: Basil Blackwell, 1985.

Ramberg, Bjorn T. *Donald Davidson's Philosophy of Language: An Introduction.* Oxford: Basil Blackwell, 1989.

Vermazen, Bruce, and Merrill B. Hintikka, eds. *Essays on Davidson: Actions and Events.* New York: Oxford University Press, 1985.

The most important distinctively American contribution to philosophy is the pragmatist tradition. In this short, lucid, and completely convincing exposition, Professor John P. Murphy begins by exploring the roots of this tradition as found in the work of Peirce, James, and Dewey, demonstrating its power and originality. Historians of philosophy will appreciate the insight Murphy brings to these figures, but the special value of this book lies in his discussion of how the pragmatist spirit has flowered in contemporary philosophy in the work of Quine, Rorty, and Davidson.

Throughout, Murphy emphasizes the logic and structure of the views held by these six philosophers and what it is they have in common that makes their work especially "pragmatist." There is no better introduction to this historical tradition and perhaps no better way into the philosophies of the contemporaries whom Murphy discusses.

Interest in pragmatist ideas is undergoing a revival at present and this book shows us why. It will be of interest to both historians of philosophy and students of contemporary philosophy.

John P. Murphy was professor of philosophy at Trinity University in San Antonio, Texas, until his death in 1987. **Richard Rorty** is professor of humanities at the University of Virginia.

INDEX